THE GLUTEN-FREE
GUIDE TO FRANCE

Maria Ann Roglieri, Ph.D.

First edition

Published by
Mari Productions, LLC
63 Fremont Rd
Sleepy Hollow, NY 10591

Visit www.gfguidefrance.com for updates and additional publications.

1.health 2.travel 3 .gluten intolerance 4. France 5. celiac restaurants 6. celiac disease 7. gluten-free 8.GF 9. gluten-free dining 10. celiac 11. Paris 12. gluten-free Paris 13. gluten-free restaurants France

ISBN 978-0-9835409-0-8

Acknowledgements: We would like to thank the following colleagues and friends for their photo contributions: Roger Levy, Gerald Friedman, Julie Clayton, Laurie Schulz, Michelle Katzman and Joe Coyne. We would also like to thank the Association Française Des Intolérants Au Gluten and the hundreds of French restaurant owners and chefs for their generous assistance in writing this book.

About the Author: Maria Roglieri is a professor of Italian at St. Thomas Aquinas College in New York. She received her MA and Ph.D. in Italian from Harvard University, and her BA in Italian from Columbia University. She and her daughter, Sara, have both been gluten-free for seven years.

In addition to *The Gluten-Free Guide*s series, Dr. Roglieri has authored *Dante and Music: Musical Adaptations of the Commedia from the 16th Century to the Present* (Ashgate Publishing, 2001) and numerous articles/chapters on Dante and music.

The Gluten-Free Guides

THE GLUTEN-FREE GUIDE TO FRANCE
www.gfguidefrance.com

is the latest in our series which also includes:

The Gluten-Free Guide to Italy
www.gfguideitaly.com

The Gluten-Free Guide to New York
www.gfguideny.com

The Gluten-Free Guide to Washington, D.C.
www.gfguidedc.com

To purchase these guides or to find out
about upcoming publications, see

www.theglutenfreeguides.com

Table of Contents

This book is dedicated with love to

David, Julia, Sara and Daniel Friedman

INTRODUCTION

When I began studying French in the sixth grade, I never imagined that someday I would be writing a travel book about France! Luckily, I had a great French teacher then and have had many others since then, as well as wonderful trips to France.

I also never imagined when I was studying French in the sixth grade that someday I would be living in a gluten-free world. My daughter Sara and I have been gluten-free for a number of years now (she has celiac disease and I have gluten neuropathy).

This book is an attempt to reciprocate some of the enormous generosity that Sara and I received when we initially went gluten-free, and that we are still receiving. It was written with the help of a large number of friends, colleagues (native French speakers, French teachers and professors), and professional restauranteurs, none of whom have celiac disease themselves but who wanted to help us and millions of other gluten-free tourists experience the joys of gluten-free France. To all of you (and you know who you are!), *merci beaucoup!*

The book is written in the spirit of "celiacs helping celiacs," because we had so many requests for it from fellow celiacs who have used the other three books in the series: *The Gluten-Free Guide to Italy*, *The Gluten-Free Guide to New York,* and *The Gluten-Free Guide to Washington, D.C.* The book offers the gluten- intolerant community a wealth of information about traveling gluten-free all over the beautiful regions of France. It presents extensive lists of, and information about, restaurants, bakeries, and health food stores that serve and sell gluten-free food all over France.

There are over 950 restaurants listed in this guide, and that is testament to how receptive to gluten-free dining the French are. We definitely received some adamant "no's" from restaurant owners when we asked if we could get a gluten-free meal, but we were very pleasantly surprised at just how many "yes, absolutely"'s we received! Many restaurant owners and chefs were very eager to work with us to ensure a memorable dining experience.

The only barrier, in fact, that we found was the language: all over France there are not as many people as one might hope who are able to speak English. And so we have included extensive vocabulary help in this book. Be sure to make use of it and you'll find many doors opened to you!

Let the reader be forewarned that *these lists are fluid*: restaurants, B&B's, and health food stores come and go. (It is a good idea to call first; for all of the restaurants in this book, phone numbers are listed.) Thus, this publication should not be considered the sole authority on the subject of dining out gluten-free or shopping for gluten-free foods in France. It is, however, to date the most complete series of lists available to the worldwide gluten-free community. The restaurants contacted by us are those recommended by fellow travelers on www.tripadvisor.com, as well as in Fodor's, Frommers, Michelin, and Zagat guidebooks.

The book will be updated periodically and for this we are counting on you: contact us after your trip to France, and let us know of any new places where you enjoyed a gluten-free meal. We will be sure to include them in the new edition!

The list of restaurants provided in the book does not represent a guarantee that food served at any restaurant is gluten free. Remember that it is always important to communicate with chefs as to your own special dietary needs. For help with this, check out the Gluten-Free French 101 section of the book.

For your convenience we have provided information, when possible, about price ranges in the restaurants listed (some restaurants do not publish prices on their websites). It must be noted, however, that in France there is a wide range of dining options in any particular restaurant. These options can vary dramatically in terms of price point. Thus, we have also included the websites of the restaurants so that you can look at the menus more closely before going to the restaurant. Most restaurants typically offer an "à la carte" menu option, as well as several fixed-price options. In order to determine the price points represented in this book, we looked at the "à la carte menu" to try to determine the average cost for a main course for 1 including 5% tax and service. Please note that menu prices are subject to change at any time, so again, it is best to consult the website of a particular restaurant.

Enjoy your trip to France, and especially enjoy the food. The landscape, the history, the culture, the art, and the people of France are all wonderful, but the food is truly divine!!

Bonnes vacances et bon appétit!

HOW TO USE THIS BOOK

The first part of the book offers information that is useful before you go to France. The second part of the book offers extensive vocabulary help for ordering GF food in France.

The third part of the book presents over 900 GF venues all over France. It is divided into **chapters** that represent each **region of France**. (With the exception of the first chapter, which is devoted entirely to Paris, and is divided by neighborhood.) The chapters are divided into **cities and towns** within each region. Gluten-free (GF) venues in this book are those we personally contacted and those recommended by fellow gluten-free travelers to France. The venues identified in each chapter are hotels and B&B's, restaurant and health food stores (*magasins bio*) and/or supermarkets that carry GF food products. There are many *magasins bio* stores in France; we have listed the ones that carry the most gluten-free products.

The following information on each venue is provided:

Name	type of venue	cuisine	price point*
Address**		phone number***	website (if any)
specialized notes			

EXAMPLE:

| **Des Si & Des Mets** | restaurant | bio |
| 63, rue Lepic, 2e. | www.dessietdesmets.com | tel. 01 42 55 19 61 |

Notes: €€€; highly recommended by celiacs all over the world.

*Price points are provided when possible (taken from the a la carte menu) for a main course for 1 incl. 5% tax and service, and are categorized as follows:

price range	symbol
Under €17	€
€18-€24	€€
€25-€32	€€€
Over €32	€€€€
Not available	N/A

**For Paris, the neighborhood number is provided after the street address.
***The phone numbers provided are from *within* France and thus do not include codes to dial out of the country of residence (varies by country) or the country code for France which is 33.

WHAT YOU NEED TO KNOW

BEFORE YOU GO

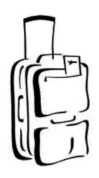

GETTING TO FRANCE: THE FLIGHT

There are a number of airlines that will provde a gluten-free meal on the flight to France. It is very important to notify the staff that you need such a meal well in advance. You can do so via their website or in person on the phone. The following is a list of airlines that currently will honor a request for a gluten-free meal:

Air Canada
Air France
American Airlines
Austrian Airlines
British Airways
Cathay Pacific
Continental Airlines
Delta Airlines
El Al
Eurowings
Finnair
Iberia
Iceland Air
LAN Airlines
Lufthansa
Luxair
Malev
Olympic Airlines
Qantas
SAS
SATA
Swiss International Airlines
TAP Air Portugal
Turkish Airlines
United Airlines
US Air
Virgin Atlantic

GETTING TO AND AROUND FRANCE: THE CRUISE

Many of the major cruise lines are able to serve customers gluten-free meals with advance notice. One cruise line that is particularly highly recommended by fellow celiacs is:

> Viking River Cruise in Northern France
> tel. 877 668-4546
> http://www.vikingrivercruises.com

This cruise line offers an 8-day cruise from Paris to Normandy and back. You can request for gluten-free food, and discuss the day's menu every morning with the maitre d' to enjoy 3 gourmet GF meals each day. If you eat at a restaurant off the ship while touring, they will make sure that the restaurant is informed ahead of time.

Other cruise lines offering gluten-free meals on trips to France include:

- Carnival Cruise Lines (tel. 800 438- 6744, www.carnival.com)

- Celebrity Cruises (tel. 800 647-2251, www.celebritycruises.com)

- Costa (tel. 800 288-6006, http://www.cruises.com/promotion/costa-cruises.do)

- Disney Cruise lines (tel. 800 951-3532, http://disneycruise.disney.go.com)

- Norwegian Cruise lines (tel. 866 234-7350, http://www2.ncl.com/)

- Princess Cruise lines (tel. 800 774-6237, www.princess.com)

- Thompson Cruise Lines (England: tel. 08712314691, www.thomson.co.uk/cruise.html)

WHEN YOU'RE THERE: LODGING OPTIONS

The lodging offered in major cities in France usually feature hotels. The higher-end hotels will offer breakfast in the restaurant setting or room service for an additional price, while the lower-end hotels will sometimes offer a continental breakfast included with the price of the room. There are some hotels listed in this book that, with advance notice, will either prepare or bring in a gluten-free breakfast for gluten-free customers. Many of these belong to the chains of **Marriott** and **Hilton**. **Keep in mind that the restaurants in the Marriotts and Hiltons will also serve gluten-free food with advance notice.**

There are also a number of all-inclusive Club Med resorts outside of the cities that will provide you with gluten-free food during the entire length of your stay. These are listed below.

The lodging in rural France, however, generally features bed-and-breakfast or **chambres d'hotes.** You can also rent a furnished house in the countryside by the week or by the month, called a **gite rural**. While the latter is useful for celiacs in that they can bring in gluten-free food purchased at health food stores, the former, B&Bs, offer very interesting possibilities because there is a multitude of B&B's that **specialize in serving the gluten-free community**.

At most of these B&B's, in addition to a great gluten-free breakfast, you can also get a delicious gluten-free dinner, cooked by and eaten with the owners. These meals are called **table d'hote dinners**. One B&B, listed in the following pages, even offers a week of gluten-free cooking classes!

The only tricky thing is that hosts of the B&B's, unlike the hosts in metropolitan hotels are less likely to speak English.

In the "Gluten-Free France by Region" sections you will find information about B&B's all over France that specialize in gluten-free; these establishments are very highly recommended by fellow celiac travelers. The basic information about these B&B's is listed on the next page.

B&B'S SPECIALIZING IN SERVING GLUTEN-FREE GUESTS:

Cherves De Cognac B-B
14 Chemin des Basses rues   Cherves Richemont (Limousin)
tel. 06 32 50 19 46   www.glutenfreefrance.com

Le Chêne Vert
34 rue des Abatis, Chez Primo   Burie (Poitou-Charentes)
tel. 05 46 90 66 96   lynneadams34@hotmail.com

Muriska Bed and Breakfast
11 rue Dongaitz Anaiak   Urrugne (Midi-Pyrénées)
tel. 06 89 43 85 26   www.muriska.com

La Belle Demeure
Lieu-dit Le Bouscot   St. Cybranet (Aquitaine)
tel. 05 53 28 57 12   www.labelledemeure.com

Chambres d'hôtes et gîte sans gluten
Marie-Laure Tauzin, Village   Montbernard (Midi-Pyrénées)
tel .05 61 94 19 60   www.chambresdhotes-sansgluten.fr/

Chambres d'hôtes à Carcassonne
Domaine Saint Louis Maquens   Carcassonne (Languedoc Roussillon)
tel. 04 68 47 52 46   www.chambresdhotes-sansgluten.fr

Château de Villars
Chateau de Villars
Pres de la cure   Villars (Aquitaine)
tel. 05 53 03 41 58   www.chateaudevillars.com/fr

CLUB MED RESORT PROPERTIES IN FRANCE
There are a number of all-inclusive Club Med properties in France that will, with advance notice, serve gluten-free meals.
Below is a list of such properties by region.
The main telephone number for Club Med in France is (33) 01 53 35 35 53.

RHONE ALPES
CLUB MED CHAMONIX HOTEL "LE SAVOY"
191 Allée Du Savoy 74400
Chamonix Cedex
tel. 4 50 53 87 80   fax: 4 50 53 33 71

CHARENTE-MARITIME
CLUB MED LA PALMYRE ATLANTIQUE
Allee Du Grand Large 17570
La Palmyre
tel. 5 46 39 77 30   fax: 5 46 02 61 66

PROVENCE
CLUB MED OPIO EN PROVENCE
Chemin Cambarnier-Nord 06650
Opio
tel. 4 93 09 71 00   fax: 4 93 09 71 70

LIMOUSIN
CLUB MED POMPADOUR
Domaine De La Noaille 19230
Arnac Pompadour
tel. 5 55 97 30 00   fax: 5 55 97 30 49

VOSGES
CLUB MED VITTEL ERMITAGE
88800 Vittel
tel. 3299088150   fax : 329088151

CLUB MED VITTEL LE PARC
88800 Vittel tel. 3 29 08 18 80   fax: 3 29 08 11 50

DISNEYLAND® PARK PARIS

If you find yourself going to Disneyland Paris, you can rest assured that there are adequate GF meals for you to consume at all of the restaurants in the park. For more detailed information about GF food available in the park, see the "Île-de-France" section of this book.

List of Disneyland® park hotels offering gluten-free meals:

Disneyland Hotel
Disney's Davy Crockett Ranch
Disney's Hotel Cheyenne
Disney's Hotel New York
Disney's Hotel Santa Fe
Disney's Newport Bay Club
Disney's Sequoia Lodge
Hotel l'Elysée Val D'Europe
Kyriad Hotel
Radisson Blu Hotel
Thomas Cook's Explorers Hotel
Vienna International Dream Castle Hotel

ASSOCIATION FRANÇAISE DES INTOLÉRANTS AU GLUTEN (AFDIAG)
(The French Association of the Gluten-Intolerant)

15 rue d'Hauteville - 75010 PARIS - FRANCE
tel: 01 56 08 08 22 / fax: 01 56 08 08 42
email: afdiag@yahoo.fr
www.afdiag.org

This association does not offer a list of restaurants that are able to provide quick free meals. It does, however, offer a number of useful things on its website including:

- a chart of foods that are forbidden and foods that are allowed

- a list of companies that produce gluten-free products and distributors of said products.

- a contact person if you need help during your trip: for a matter of great urgency Catherine Remillieux-Rast can answer you if she is home; if not, just leave a message and she can try to call you back. The telephone (or fax) number is 01 30 99 36 68 when you are in France, and 33 1 30 99 36 68 from another country.

WHERE TO FIND PREPACKAGED GF PRODUCTS:

You will find gluten-free products in pharmacies, *magasin bio* or *bio* health food stores, or in dietetic food stores *magasins de produits de régime.* **We have listed the biggest of these venues alongside our list of restaurants for each region (see the section "France by Region".)**

Some supermarkets such as MONOPRIX, CASINO, AUCHAN, CARREFOUR, now have gluten free products but you are probably better off going to the *bio* stores where you will find a greater selections of gluten-free products including muesli, cereals, muffins, small cakes and cookies.

In these stores you will find many products by such companies as VALPIFORM, BIAGLUT & SCHAER, GLUTABYE, and NATURE ET COMPAGNIE.

Most of those brands make sliced breads, pastas, noodles, biscuits, flour, and cakes (*pain tranché, pâtes, nouilles, biscuits, farines,* and *gateaux* respectively) gluten-free (*sans gluten*).

Some products that celiacs have recommended highly are the following:

- VALPIFORM baguettes, croissants, pain au chocolate and madeline cakes
- Barket pretzels

In the store look for this sign on the products or just "SG":

One of the best pharmacies/bio stores to go to in Paris is Biosphare:

57, rue Saint Maur 75011 Paris
Tél/fax : 01 48 06 08 81
M° Rue Saint-Maur

Mardi au vendredi 9h30 - 13h & 14h30 - 19h30
Lundi 14h30 - 19h30 / Samedi 9h30 - 13h

UN MONDE SANS GLUTEN...

**SANS GLUTEN - VEGETARIEN - FRUITS & LEGUMES - FRAIS - VINS
PETITS PRODUCTEURS - ECO PRODUITS**

- FRUITS et LEGUMES biologiques de saison, en provenance de France
- PRODUITS SANS GLUTEN
- PRODUITS VEGETARIENS
- Rayon FRAIS
- Vins DIRECT PRODUCTEUR en culture biologique et biodynamique
- Produits issus de nos campagnes et achetés en direct à des
  PETITS PRODUCTEURS

Crée en octobre 2006 par Frédéric Slonina, le magasin offre un grand choix de produits sans gluten : Schär, Valpiform, France Aglut Bio, La Finestra sul Cielo, Proceli, Hubmann, Schnitzer, Pural, Probios, Ma vie sans gluten, Les Recettes de Céliane, Damhert...

A WORD ABOUT GLUTEN-FREE BREADS IN FRANCE

There are typically several types of bread that you can find that are gluten free:

- white bread, typically called a *baguette*
- whole-wheat like rolls such as *Sunna* by Schar
- country-style bread *pain campagnard* by France Aglut, GlutaBye and Valpiform
- German-style rye-like organic buckwheat and whole grain breads made from not only buckwheat but also combinations of corn, sunflower seeds, millet, soy, rice, beans, apples and honey. Check out Bio Kerniges Buchweizenbrot, Glutenfrieies Volkombrot.

Some local bakers will make gluten-free breads and sell them in the *bio* stores. The bio store **Naturalia**, for example carries 4 kinds of gluten-free breads that are made fresh every day: *chataignier* (chestnut), teff, quinoa, & *sarrasin* (buckwheat). The restaurant **Des Si et Des Mes** in Paris, an extremely popular favorite among celiacs, will also sell their fresh gluten-free bread as a takeout order.

You can order **fresh** gluten-free products, as fresh bread (*pain frais*), fresh baguettes and fresh cakes (*gâteaux*), by telephoning or mailing to:

1. VALPIFORM: www.valpiform.com

2. Soreda Diet (Glutabye products)
   2 impasse des Crêts,
   74960 Cran Gevrier
   tel: 04 50 57 73 99
   fax: 04 50 57 88 45
   www.glutabye.com

A WORD ABOUT GLUTEN-FREE DESSERTS IN FRANCE

There are several types of delicious gluten-free desserts that you can easily find in France:

- *Galettes* are made with only buckwheat flour (*blè noir* or *farine sarrasin*). They are like crepes but are GF and are served open faced. There are many creperies in Paris which advertise *galettes de sarrasin* (make sure to confirm that they are *sans gluten* (gluten-free) or *seulement avec sarrasin* (only with buckwheat flour).

  Two of the most popular places in Paris to enjoy *galettes* are: **Aux Ducs de Bourgogne** (just around the corner from the Museè Rodin) and **Breizh Café** (in Marais).

- A *flottante* is a giant meringue floating in creme anglaise. They can be found in bakeries all over France.

- *Macaroon*s are chewy cookies made with sugar, egg whites, and almond paste or coconut. They can be found in bakeries all over France.

If you find yourself in Etivey in the region of Burgundy, you MUST go to an exclusively gluten-free bakery:

Aux Biscuits d'Antoine
5, petite rue, Etivey in the region of Burgundy
tel. 330386557173
http://biscuits-antoine.com

This is perhaps the only gluten-free bakery in all of France and is well worth the trip. Some of the *bio* stores carry their cookies as well.

CHAINS IN FRANCE OFFERING GLUTEN-FREE OPTIONS

FAST FOOD/FOOD TO GO

Exki
Is a restaurant chain that sells fast, healthy
foods. It has marked SG (sans gluten) on the
labels of some of their products.

Cojean
This establishment provides GF soups and salads to go and has quite a
following among celiacs.

RESTAURANT CHAINS

These are two popular restaurant chains in France. We contacted the quality
control people at the central office to find out if it would be possible to get a
gluten-free meal in these establishments. The following is information that
they provided:

We have 9 gluten-free recipes :
- Entries = "les crevettes parmentières"
- Mussels = "les mini-moules", "les moules
à l'escargot gratinées", "le grand poëlon de
Noël (only for Christmas period)", and "les
moules en papillotes au saumon basilic"
- Desserts = "ananas frais", "Glace
Liégeoise au café", "glace liégeoise au
chocolat", "le fromage blanc".

All of our recipes are cooked in our kitchen so there is a risk of cross
contaminations between the gluten-free products and those which contain
gluten traces or gluten.

Buffalo Grill is a steakhouse chain that provides a list to its staff regarding the presence of allergens in the meals. As a result, if you ask the staff for gluten-free, they will be able to provide you with a gluten-free meal. The list is not readily available to patrons. You can show the staff the following excerpt from an email the Director of Quality Control sent us which essentially explains this:

Pour répondre à votre demande, notre service qualité central établit tous les mois un bilan des allergènes majeurs (tels que définis dans la règlementation Européenne - Directive CE 2003/89) présents dans l'ensemble des produits et plats proposés.

Ces éléments ne sont pas diffusés à notre clientèle mais sont disponibles (sous forme de fiches) pour consultation au sein de l'ensemble de nos restaurants Buffalo Grill et permettent à chaque client allergique d'identifier les produits qu'il peut consommer.

Cependant cette information ne tient pas compte des éventuelles contaminations croisées survenues chez nos fournisseurs et lors de l'élaboration dans nos restaurants.

Aussi, nous invitons notre clientèle à consulter les fiches allergènes et à prévenir le serveur (se) de leur intolérance, celui-ci saura les conseiller et les guider lors de leur commande sur des produits qui leur correspondent.

Restant à votre entière disposition pour plus d'informations.

Bien cordialement,

Estelle
Service Consommateurs

GLUTEN-FREE FRENCH 101:

MAKING RESERVATIONS

AND

REQUESTING A GLUTEN-FREE MEAL

en francais

DINING OUT: MAKING RESERVATIONS
AND REQUESTING A GLUTEN-FREE MEAL

Many French restaurant managers and chefs are very familiar with gluten-free customers and are willing to serve them gourmet gluten-free meals. **They do strongly request, however, that you make reservations and request a gluten-free meal in advance,** both because restaurants get very crowded and thus it is necessary to reserve a table, and because they would like to be sure to have fresh ingredients on hand to serve a gluten-free meal. We cannot emphasize enough the importance of making a reservation in these restaurants. There are some restaurant owners who have indicated that reservations are not necessary; these are indicated in the text of this book.

In order to assist you in making reservations and requesting a gluten-free meal, we have provided vocabulary help in this section. In addition, in the back of the book is an extensive glossary for help with reading the menus.

You can do this by phone, e-mail or fax or through the online reservation services such as:

www.lafourchette.com
www.bookatable.com
www.toptable.com

MAKING RESERVATIONS
(phonetic pronunciation help in parentheses)

Good day, madame/sir. I would like to reserve a table for _____ people, please.

> **Bonjour, madame /monsieur. Je voudrais réserver une table pour **_____ personnes, s'il vous plaît.**
> (Bo n geor madame/missur, ge voodray reservay oohn tahble poor ____ personne, sill vooh play.)

I would like to request a gluten-free meal for _____ people, please.

> **Je voudrais demander un repas sans gluten pour ** _____ personnes, s'il vous plaît.**
> (Ge voodray demanday uhn raypa son glutenne poor ____ personne, sill vooh play.)

**1 un (uhn), 2 deux (deuh), 3 trois (twah), 4 quattre (kaht-ruh), 5 cinque (sank), 6 six (siis), 7 sept (set), 8 huit (wheat!!), 9 neuf (nuf), 10 dix (diis)

Thank you very much madame/sir.

> **Merci beaucoup, madame/monsieur.**
> (Merci bowcoop, madame/monsieur.)

MEALS
le petit déjeuner breakfast   **le déjeuner**   lunch
le diner   dinner

MENUS

le menu   fixed-price menu   **la carte**   regular menu

Of the more than 900 restaurants in this book, only a few offer a specific gluten-free menu. So once you're at the restaurant, you need to explain to the manager, waiter, and/or chef precisely what your dietary needs are. You can use the words in the box on the next page ("Celiac Identification Card") or the longer version which follows, provided by the French Celiac Society.

CELIAC IDENTIFICATION CARD
FOR THE CHEF AND WAITER
(Translations on next page)

J'ai la maladie coeliaque et pour des raisons médicales je dois manger des aliments SANS GLUTEN. Je peux manger la nourriture qui a le riz, le maïs, les pommes de terre, de légumes et de fruits tout, des oeufs, du fromage, du lait, la viande, le poisson, tant qu'elle n'a pas été préparée avec la farine, la chapelure ou de la sauce contenant du blé ou du gluten. Je ne peux pas manger des aliments contenant de la farine de blé ou de céréales (kamut, épeautre, duram, semoule, et bulgar), le seigle, l'orge ou du gluten. Merci pour votre aide.

Translations of Celiac Identification Card:

E = English, D = Deutsch, S = Español, I = Italiano

E) I have celiac disease and for medical reasons I have to eat food WITHOUT GLUTEN. I can eat food that has rice, corn, potatoes, vegetables and any fruit, eggs, cheese, milk, meat, fish, as long as it has not been prepared with flour, breadcrumbs or sauce containing wheat or gluten. I can not eat food containing wheat flour or cereal (kamut, spelt, duram, semolina, and bulger), rye, barley, or gluten. Thank you for your help.

(D) Ich habe Zöliakie und ich muss Lebensmittel OHNE GLUTEN essen. Ich kann Reis, Mais, Kartoffeln, Gemüse und Obst, Eier, Käse, Milch, Fleisch, Fisch essen, solange sie noch nicht mit Mehl, Paniermehl oder Sauce mit Weizen oder Gluten zu bereitet sind. Ich kann nicht Lebensmittel mit Weizen Mehl oder Getreide (Kamut, Dinkel, langsamer, Grieß und Bulgarisch), Roggen, Gerste, oder Gluten essen. Vielen Dank für Ihre Hilfe.

(I) Sono celiaco e devo mangaiare cibo SENZA GLUTINE. Posso mangiare il cibo che ha riso, mais, patate, ortaggi e qualsiasi frutta, uova, formaggio, latte, carne, pesce, purchè non sia stato preparato con farina, pangrattato, o salsa che contiene frumento o glutine.Non posso mangiare il cibo che contiene farine di grano o di cereali (kamut, spelta, duram, semola, e bulgar), segale, orzo, o glutine. Grazie per il Suo aiuto.

(S) Tengo la enfermedad que se llama celiaca y tengo que comer alimentos SIN GLUTEN. Puedo comer alimentos que contienen arroz, maíz, papas, vegetales y cualquier tipo de fruta. También, puedo comer alimentos que contienen huevos, queso, leche, carne, y pescado, siempre que no hayan sido preparados con harina, pan, salsa o que contengan gluten de trigo. No puedo comer alimentos que contengan harina de trigo o cereales (kamut, escanda, duram, sémola, y bulgar), centeno, cebada, o gluten. Gracias por su ayuda.

COPY OF ASSOCIATION FRANÇAISE DES INTOLÉRANTS AU GLUTEN (AFDIAG) MEMBERSHIP CARD
(provided to us by the secretary of the organization)

Le possesseur de cette carte est une personne souffrant de la MALADIE COELIAQUE. LE SEUL TRAITEMENT DE LA MALADIE COELIAQUE consiste à suivre un régime STRICT SANS GLUTEN.

LE RÉGIME SANS GLUTEN
En tant qu'intolérant au gluten, **JE NE DOIS PAS MANGER** d'aliment contenant du BLÉ (ou FROMENT, KAMUT, ÉPEAUTRE), du TRITICALE, de l'ORGE, de l'AVOINE, du SEIGLE car ils contiennent TOUS du GLUTEN. Même une infime quantité de ces derniers me rendrait malade.

ALIMENTS INTERDITS
Les farines de blé, orge, avoine, seigle et leurs dérivés, ainsi que les pains, croissants, brioches, gâteaux, tartes, biscuits, pizzas, quiches, nouilles et pâtes diverses, certaines soupes, les sauces et les crèmes faites à base de farine de blé, les biscuits apéritifs, la chapelure, …

SOURCES CACHÉES DU GLUTEN
Amidon de blé, amidon de blé modifié, extrait de malt, malt. Ces ingrédients peuvent se trouver dans certains bouillons cubes, soupes déshydratées, fonds de sauces, charcuterie, épices, sauce soja, assaisonnements.

ATTENTION AUX MÉDICAMENTS
Vérifiez la nature de l'excipient.

ALIMENTS SANS DANGER
Viandes et poissons natures, grillés ou bouillis, fruits, légumes, oeufs, ainsi que les riz, maïs, soja, sarrasin, tapioca et produits à base de pomme de terre.

EXPLANATIONS OF CELIAC DISEASE IN DIFFERENT LANGUAGES
(provided to us by the AFDIAG)

FRANÇAIS: "Il m'est interdit de manger des produits contenant du froment (blé), du seigle, de l'orge ou de l'avoine, donc également ce qui est pané ou lié avec de la farine. Le maïs, le riz, les pommes de terre, les légumes, les viandes, etc. ... me sont permis, ainsi que les soupes et les sauces liées avec de l'amidon (de maïs) ou avec de la fécule de pomme de terre."

ANGLAIS: "For medical reasons, I am not allowed to eat any products made of wheat, rye, barley, or oat and nothing breaded or thickened with flour. I may eat maize, rice, potatoes, vegetables, meat, etc ... as well as soups and gravies thickened with starch of maize or potato flour."

ALLEMAND: "Ich darf aus medizinischen Gründen keine Produkte aus Weisen, Roggen, Gerste oder Hafer essen, also auch nichts Paniertes oder Mehl-Gebundenes. Mais, Reis, Kartoffeln, Gemüse, Fleisch usw. sind erlaubt, auch Suppen und Saucen, die mit Speisestärkeoder Kartoffelmehl gebunden sind".

ESPAGNOL: "Por orden médica me esta prohibido ingerir alimentas que deriven de trigo, avena, cebada y centeno por Io tanto nada que sea apanado o espesado con harina. Maiz, arroz, patatas, verduras, carne, etc. estan permidos en mi dicta, asi también sopas y salsas espemdas con maicena o harina de patatas."

ITALIEN: "Per ragioni medicali mi è vietato di mangiare prodotti fatti di grano, di segale, d'orzo o d'avena dunque niente che sia preparato con farina o panato. Sono permessi mais, riso, patate, legumi, carne, etc ... e anche minestre e salse legati ai amido."

May I please speak to the chef?
Puis-je parler au chef, s'il vous

gluten-free
sans gluten

GENERAL QUESTIONS TO ASK
IN THE RESTAURANT
(provided to us by the AFDIAG)

Can you please help me choose a gluten-free meal from the menu?
I need your advice.

> **S'il vous plaît pouvez m'aider à choisir dans le menu un repas sans gluten? Vos conseils me sont nécessaires.**

Please could you tell me if this dish contain any wheat flour?

> **Pourriez-vous m'indiquer si la farine de blé entre dans la composition de ce plat ?**

. . . without sauce please?

> **. . . sans sauce, s'il vous plait?**

I have to eat special bread. Can you toast this bread for me please ?

> **Je dois manger un pain spécial. Pouvez-vous faire griller ce pain s'il vous plaît ?**

# MORE SPECIFIC QUESTIONS
# FOR THE CHEF OR WAITER
D = Deutsch
S = Español, I = Italiano
English in regular print
French in bold print

Is this dish coated in wheat flour or breadcrumbs before it is cooked?

(I) questo piattoè impanato di farina di frumento o molliche di pane prima che sia cotto?
(D) Ist das Gericht paniert mit Weizenmehl, bevor es gekocht wird?
(Sp) ¿Está este plato preparado con pan rallado o harina de trigo?

Est-ce que ce plat est pané ou préparé avec de la farine avant sa cuisson?

Is this dish preseasoned or cooked in broth or bouillon?

(I) È questo piatto condito o cotto in brodo o bouillion?
(D) Ist das Gericht gewürzt oder gekocht in Brühe oder Bouillon?
(Sp) ¿Está sazonado o cocinado el plato con caldo?

Est-ce que ce plat est cuit ou préparé avec du bouillon?

If it is preseasoned or cooked with boullion is there any wheat, rye, barley, or gluten in the seasoning or in the boullion?

(I) Se si utilizzano condimenti confezionati in imballaggi o brodo o bouillion, non vi è alcun grano, segale, orzo, o glutine nel miscuglio?
(D) Wenn Sie verpackt Gewürze oder Brühe oder vorgefertigten bouillion, gebrauchen gibt es eine Weizen, Roggen, Gerste, oder Gluten Mischung?
(Sp) Si utilizó condimentos envasados o caldo, ¿ contienen trigo, centeno, cebada, gluten o una mezcla de estos ingredientes?

Si vous utilisez des assaisonnements emballés ou préemballés avec du bouillon, y at-il de blé, du seigle, de l'orge ou du gluten dans le mélange?

Is this dish fried in the same fryer where wheat dishes are fried?

(I) È questo piatto fritto nella stessa friggitrice dove i piatti di grano sono fritti?
(D) Ist das Gericht gebraten in der gleichen Friteuse, wie die speisehaus Weizer?
(Sp) ¿Se frió este plato en la misma sartén en que se fríen platos que contienen trigo?

Est-ce que ce plat frit dans la même friteuse que des plats frits avec la farine?

Is this dish thickened with flour?

(I) Questo piatto è ispessito con farina?
(D) Ist das Gericht mit Mehl verdickt?
(Sp) ¿Se ha espesado el plato con harina?

Ce plat est-il épaissi à la farine?

French	English	Spanish	Italian	German
poisson	fish	pescado	pesce	fisch
viande	meat	carne	carne	fleisch
haricots	beans	frijol	legumi	bohnen
legumes	vegetables	vegetales	verdura	gemüse
fruits	fruit	frutas	frutta	obst

SAFE AND UNSAFE INGREDIENTS

UNSAFE INGREDIENTS

French	English	Spanish	Italian	German
farine	flour	harina	farina	meh
blé	wheat	trigo	frumento	weize
amidon de blé	wheat starch	fecula de trigo	amido di frumento	weizenstärk
farine de blé	wheat flour	harina de trigo	farina di frumento	weizenmel
orge	barley	cebada	orzo	gerst
froment	rye	centeno	segale	rogge
pain	bread	pan	pane	br
chapelure	breadcrumbs	pan rallado	pane grattugiato	paniermel
semoule	semolina	sémola	semolina	grie

SAFE INGREDIENTS

French	English	Spanish	Italian	German
avoine	oats	avena	avena	hafer
riz	rice	arroz	riso	reis
l'amidon de riz	rice starch	fecula de arroz	amido di ris	reisstärke
farine de riz	rice flour	harina de arroz	farina di riso	reismehl
pomme de terre	potatoes	papa	patate	kartoffel
farine de pommes	potato flour	harina de papa	fecola di patate	kartoffel-mehl
maïs dous	corn	maiz dulce	mais	mais
fécule de maïs	cornstarch	de maicena	amido di mais	maisstärke
farine de tapioca	tapioca	harina de tapioca	farina di tapioca	tapioca mehl
farine de châtaigne	chestnut flour	harina de castaña	farina di castagne	kastanienmehl
farine d'almande	almond flour	harina de almendra	farina di mandorle	mandel-mehl
farine de soja	soy flour	haina de soja	farina di soia	soja-mehl

USEFUL PHRASES FOR BUYING GF FOOD PRODUTS IN THE STORE
(provided by the Association Française Des Intolérants Au Gluten)

- I am a celiac/gluten-intolerant. This means I become ill if I eat anything containing wheat, oats, barley or rye flour.

  Je suis intolérant au gluten. C'est-à-dire que je suis malade si je mange une préparation contenant de la farine de blé, d'avoine, d'orge ou de seigle.

- Does this product contain wheat, oats, barley or rye?

  Ce produit contient-il du blé, de l'avoine, de l'orge ou du seigle?

- Do you sell gluten-free foods?

  Vendez-vous des produits sans gluten?

- I would like to buy some gluten-free foods.

  J'aimerais acheter des produits sans gluten.

FOOD WORDS DICTIONARY IN MULTIPLE LANGUAGES

- **FRENCH TO ENGLISH AND GERMAN**
- **FRENCH TO SPANISH AND ITALIAN**

French	English	German
À la soude	with soda	Mit Soda
Abricot	apricot	Aprikose
Ail	garlic	Knoblauch
Almond farine	almond flour	Mandel-Mehl
Amidon de blé	wheat starch	Weizenstärke
Ananas	pineapple	Ananas
Apple	apple	Apple
Avec du lait	with milk	Mit Milch
Avec jambon et fromage	with ham and cheese	Mit Schinken und Käse
Avoine	oats	Hafer
Baked	baked	Gebacken
Banane	banana	Banane
Battues avec des œufs et des miettes de pain frit et	battered with eggs and bread crumbs and fried	Verbeulte mit Eiern und Semmelbrösel und gebratene
Bébé agneau	baby lamb	Baby Lamb
Beurre	butter	Butter
Bien fait	well done	Well done
Bière	beer	Bier
Blé	wheat	Weizen
Bleuets	blueberries	Blaubeeren
Boire	drink	Trinken
Boire	drink	Trinken
Bouteille	bottle	Flasche
Bovine	veal	Kalbfleisch
Café	coffee	Kaffee
Canard	duck	Ente
Carafe	carafe	Karaffe

French	English	German
Carotte	carrot	Karotte
Carte des vins	wine list	Weinkarte
Cassis	black currant	Schwarze Johannisbeere
Cerveau	brain	Gehirn
Chapelure	breadcrumbs	Paniermehl
Chef	chef	Küchenchef
Cherry	cherry	Cherry
Chocolat chaud	hot chocolate	Heiße Schokolade
Chou	cabbage	Kohl
Chou-fleur	cauliflower	Blumenkohl
Cidre	cider	Apfelwein
Citron	lemon	Zitrone
Clair / foncé	light/dark	Hell / Dunkel
Coeliaque	celiac	Celiac
Concombre	cucumber	Gurke
Cookies	cookies	Cookies
Côtes d'agneau	lamb chop	Lamm-Kotelett
Couvrir les frais	cover charge	Cover charge
Crabe	crab	Krabbe
Crème glacée	ice cream	Eis
Crêpe	pancake	Pfannkuchen
Crevettes / crevettes	prawns / shrimps	Garnelen / Shrimps
Croissant	croissant	Croissant
Crus avec du citron et l'oeuf	raw with lemon and egg	Roh mit Zitrone und Ei
Dans la saison	in season	In der Saison
Dates	dates	Termine
De fromage parmesan et tomates	with Parmesan cheese and tomatoes	Mit Parmesan-Käse und Tomaten

French	English	German
De la crème...	cream of . . .	Sahne. . .
Déjeuner	lunch	Mittagessen
Dîner	dinner	Abendessen
Eau	water	Wasser
Eau minérale	mineral water	Mineralwasser
Eau minérale	mineral water	Mineralwasser
Faisan	pheasant	Fasan
Farcis	stuffed	Ausgestopft
Farine	flour	Mehl
Farine de blé	wheat flour	Weizenmehl
Farine de châtaigne	chestnut flour	Kastanienmehl
Farine de pommes de terre ou amidon	potato flour/starch	Kartoffel-Mehl / Stärke
Farine de riz	rice flour	Reismehl
Farine de soja	soy flour	Soja-Mehl
Farine de tapioca	tapioca flour	Tapioka Mehl
Fécule de maïs	cornstarch	Maisstärke
Figues	figs	Feigen
Fiscale	tax	Steuer
Foie	liver	Leber
Fraise	strawberry	Erdbeere
Framboise	raspberry	Himbeere
Framboises	raspberries	Himbeeren
Frit	fried	Fried
Frites	fries	Pommes frites
Froid, avec du vinaigre	cold, with vinegar	Kälte, mit Essig
Fruits	fruit	Obst
Fruits de mer	seafood	Meeresfrüchte
Fruits frais	fresh fruit	Frischobst

French	English	German
Fruits secs	dried fruit	Trockenfrüchte
Fumé	smoked	Geräucherte
Gâteau	cake	Kuchen
Grillé	grilled	Gegrillt
Ham	ham	Schinken
Hareng	herring	Hering
Haricots verts	green beans	Grüne Bohnen
Homard	lobster	Hummer
Hot-dog	hot dog	Hot dog
Je voudrais	I would like	Ich möchte
Jus d'ananas	pineapple juice	Ananassaft
Jus de pomme	apple juice	Apfelsaft
Jus de tomate	tomato juice	Tomatensaft
Jus d'orange	orange juice	Orangensaft
Lait	milk	Milch
Laitue	lettuce	Kopfsalat
Lamb	lamb	Lamm
L'amidon de riz	rice starch	Reisstärke
Lapin	rabbit	Kaninchen
Légumes	vegetables	Gemüse
Les huîtres	oysters	Austern
Limonade	lemonade	Limonade
Maïs doux (maïs)	sweet corn (maize)	Mais (Mais)
Melon	melon	Melone
Menu	menu	Menü
Menu fixe	fixed menu	Festnetz-Menü
Merci	thank you	Danke
Morue	cod	Kabeljau
Moules	mussels	Muscheln

French	English	German
Mousse au chocolat	chocolate mousse	Mousse au Chocolat
Moutarde	mustard	Senf
Moyen steak	medium steak	Steak medium
Mûres	blackberries	Brombeeren
Mushroom	mushroom	Pilz
Nectarine	nectarine	Nektarine
Oignon	onion	Zwiebel
Omelette	omelette	Omelett
Orange	orange	Orange
Orge	barley	Gerste
Pain	bread	Brot
Pamplemousse	grapefruit	Grapefruit
Pastèque	watermelon	Wassermelone
Pate	pate	Pate
Pâtisseries	pastries	Gebäck
Peach	peach	Peach
Petit déjeuner	breakfast	Frühstück
Petits pois	peas	Erbsen
Pieuvre	octopus	Kraken
Pizza	pizza	Pizza
Plie	plaice	Scholle
Plum	plum	Pflaume
Poire	pear	Birne
Poire	pear	Birne
Poireau	leek	Leek
Poisson	fish	Fisch
Poivre	pepper	Pfeffer
Pomme de terre	potato	Kartoffel

French	English	German
Pork chop	pork chop	Schweinskotelett
Poulet	chicken	Huhn
Pruneau	prune	Pflaume
Radis	radish	Rettich
Ragoût de poisson	fish stew	Fisch-Eintopf
Raisin	grape	Traube
Raisins secs	raisins	Rosinen
Rare steak	rare steak	Seltene Steak
Red currant	red currant	Rote Johannisbeere
Rice	Rice	Rice
Rôti de porc	pork roast	Schweinefleisch Braten
Rye	rye	Roggen
S'il vous plaît	please	Bitte
S'il vous plaît	please	Bitte
Salade de fruits	fruit salad	Obstsalat
Salade de fruits de mer	seafood salad	Meeresfrüchte-Salat
Salade verte	green salad	Grüner Salat
Sanglier	boar	Wildschwein
Sans gluten	gluten-free	Glutenfrei
Sauce	sauce	Sauce
Saumon	salmon	Lachs
Sel	salt	Salz
Semoule	semolina	Grieß
Serveuse	waitress	Kellnerin
Snack	snack	Snack
Sorbet	sherbet	Limonade
Soupe	soup	Suppe
Soupe aux légumes	vegetable soup	Gemüsesuppe

French	English	German
Spécialité de la maison	specialty of House	Spezialität des Hauses
Spécialité locale	local specialty	Lokale Spezialität
Squid	squid	Squid
Steak de boeuf	beef steak	Rind-Steak
Straight	straight	Geradeaus
Supplément / charge	extra fee/charge	Zuschlag / kostenlos
Sur les rochers	on the rocks	On the rocks
Tangerine	tangerine	Tangerine
Tarte	pie	Pie
Tasse de crème glacée	cup of ice cream	Cup of ice cream
Thé	tea	Tee
Tomate	tomato	Tomaten
Torréfié	roasted	Geröstet
Très rare	very rare	Sehr selten
Très rare steak	very rare steak	Sehr selten Steak
Truite	trout	Forelle
Un verre d'...	a glass of ...	Ein Glas...
Une bouteille d'...	a bottle of ...	Eine Flasche...
Vin blanc	white wine	Weißwein
Vin doux	sweet wine	Süßer Wein
Vin rouge	red wine	Rotwein
Vin sec	dry wine	Trockener Wein
Vinaigre	vinegar	Essig
Waiter	waiter	Kellner
Well done steak	well done steak	Well done steak
Yogourt	yogurt	Joghurt

French	Italian	Spanish
À la soude	con seltz	Con soda
Abricot	albicocca	Albaricoque
Ail	aglio	Ajo
Almond farine	farina di mandorle	De harina de almendra
Amidon de blé	amido di frumento	Almidón de trigo
Ananas	ananas	Piña
Apple	mela	Apple
Avec du lait	con latte	Con leche
Avec jambon et fromage	alla valdostana	Con jamón y queso
Avoine	avena	Avena
Baked	al forno	Horneados
Banane	banana	Plátano
Battues avec des œufs et des miettes de pain frit et	alla milanese	Maltratadas con huevos y pan rallado y frito
Bébé agneau	abbacchio	Cordero bebé
Beurre	burro	Mantequilla
Bien fait	ben cotta	Bien hecho
Bière	la birra	Cerveza
Blé	frumento	Trigo
Bleuets	mirtilli	Arándanos
Boire	bevanda	Beber
Boire	bibita	Beber
Bouteille	bottiglia	Botella
Bovine	vitello	Vacuno
Café	caffè	Café
Canard	anatra	Pato
Carotte	carota	Zanahoria

French	Italian	Spanish
Carte des vins	lista dei vini	Carta de vinos
Cassis	ribes nero	Negro currant
Cerveau	cervella	Cerebro
Chapelure	pane grattugiato	Pan
Chef	cuoco	Chef
Cherry	ciliegia	Cherry
Chocolat chaud	cioccolata calda	Chocolate caliente
Chou	cavolo	Repollo
Chou-fleur	cavolfiore	Coliflor
Cidre	sidro	Sidra
Citron	limone	Limón
Clair / foncé	chiara/scura	Luz / oscuridad
Coeliaque	celiaca	Celiaca
Concombre	cetriolo	Pepino
Cookies	biscotti	Cookies
Côtes d'agneau	Un pezzo d'agnello	Lamb chop
Couvrir les frais	coperto	Cubrir cargo
Crabe	granchio	Cangrejo
Crème glacée	gelato	Helado
Crêpe	focaccia	Pancake
Crevettes / crevettes	scampi /gamberi	Camarones / gambas
Croissant	cornetto/brioche	Croissant
Crus avec du citron et l'oeuf	alla tartara	Crudo con limón y huevo
Dans la saison	di stagione	En la temporada
Dates	datteri	Fechas
De fromage parmesan et tomates	alla parmigiana	Con queso parmesano y tomates

French	Italian	Spanish
Déjeuner	pranzo	Almuerzo
Dîner	cena	Cena
Eau	acqua	Agua
Eau minérale	acqua minerale	Agua mineral
Faisan	fagiano	Faisanes
Farcis	ripieno	De peluche
Farine	farina	Harina
Farine de blé	farina di frumento	Harina de trigo
Farine de châtaigne	farina di castagne	Harina de castaña
Farine de pommes de terre ou amidon	fecola di patate	Harina de papa o almidón
Farine de riz	farina di riso	Harina de arroz
Farine de soja	farina di soia	Harina de soja
Farine de tapioca	farina di tapioca	Harina de tapioca
Fécule de maïs	amido di mais	De maicena
Figues	fichi	Higos
Fiscale	tasse	Fiscal
Foie	fegato	Hígado
Fraise	fragola	Fresa
Framboise	lamponi	Frambuesa
Framboises	lamponi	Frambuesas
Frit	fritto	Frito
Frites	patatine fritte	Fritas
Froid, avec du vinaigre	in carpione	Fría, con vinagre
Fruits	frutta	Frutas
Fruits de mer	frutti di mare	Mariscos
Fumé	affumicato	Ahumado

French	Italian	Spanish
Grillé	alla griglia	La parrilla
Grillé	alla griglia	La parrilla
Ham	prosciutto	Ham
Hareng	aringa	Arenque
Haricots verts	fagiolini	Judías verdes
Homard	aragosta	Langosta
Hot-dog	hot dog	Perro caliente
Je voudrais	vorrei	Me gustaría
Jus d'ananas	succo d'ananas	Jugo de piña
Jus de pomme	succo di mela	Jugo de manzana
Jus de tomate	succo di pomodoro	Zumo de tomate
Jus d'orange	succo d'arancia	Jugo de naranja
Lait	latte	Leche
Laitue	lattuga	Lechuga
Lamb	agnello	Cordero
L'amidon de riz	amido di riso	Almidón de arroz
Lapin	coniglio	Conejo
Légumes	verdura	Hortalizas
Les huîtres	ostriche	Ostras
Limonade	limonata	Limonada
Maïs doux (maïs)	mais	Maíz dulce (maíz)
Melon	melone	Melón
Menu	menu	Menú
Menu fixe	prezzo fisso	Menú fijo
Merci	grazie	Gracias
Morue	merluzzo	Bacalao
Moules	cozze	Mejillones

French	Italian	Spanish
Moutarde	senape	Mostaza
Moyen steak	bistecca a media cottura	Filete mediano
Mûres	more	Moras
Mushroom	funghi	De setas
Nectarine	nocepesca	Nectarine
Oignon	cipolla	Cebolla
Omelette	omelette / frittata	Tortilla
Orange	arancia	Orange
Orge	orzo	Cebada
Pain	pane grattugiato	Pan
Pamplemousse	pompelmo	Pomelo
Pastèque	anguria	Sandía
Pate	pate'	Pate
Pâtisseries	paste	Pasteles
Peach	pesca	Peach
Petit déjeuner	colazione	Desayuno
Petits pois	piselli	Guisantes
Pieuvre	polpo	Pulpo
Pizza	pizza	Pizza
Plie	sogliola	Solla
Plum	prugna	Plum
Poire	pera	Pera
Poire	pera	Pera
Poireau	porro	Leek
Poisson	pesce	Pescado
Poivre	pepe	Pimienta

French	Italian	Spanish
Pomme de terre	patate	Papa
Pork chop	Un pezzo di maiale	Tajada de carne de cerdo
Poulet	pollo	Pollo
Pruneau	prugna secca	Podar
Radis	rafano	Rábano
Ragoût de poisson	zuppa di pesce	Guiso de pescado
Raisin	uva	De uva
Raisins secs	uva passa	Pasas
Rare steak	bistecca al sangue	Rara bistec
Red currant	ribes	Roja currant
Rice	riso	Arroz
Rôti de porc	arista	Cerdo asado
Rye	segale	Centeno
S'il vous plaît	per favore	por favor
Salade de fruits	macedonia di frutta	Ensalada de frutas
Salade de fruits de mer	in insalata	Ensalada de marisco
Salade verte	insalata	Ensalada verde
Sanglier	cinghiale	Jabalí
Sans gluten	senza glutine	Sin gluten
Sauce	salsa	Salsa
Saumon	salmone	Salmón
Sel	sale	Sal
Semoule	semolina	Sémola
Serveuse	cameriera	Camarera
Snack	spuntino	Merienda

French	Italian	Spanish
Soupe	zuppa	Sopa
Soupe aux légumes	minestrone	Sopa de verduras
Spécialité de la maison	specialita' di casa	Especialidad de la casa
Spécialité locale	specialita' locale	Especialidad local
Squid	calamari	Calamar
Steak de boeuf	bistecca	El sector de la carne de bistec
Straight	liscio	Recto
Supplément / charge	extra	Suplemento / cargo
Sur les rochers	con ghiaccio	En las rocas
Tangerine	mandarino	Mandarina
Tarte	crostata	Pastel
Tasse de crème glacée	coppa gelato	Copa de helado
Thé	te	Té
Tomate	pomodoro	Tomate
Torréfié	arrosto	Asado
Très rare	al sangue	Muy raro
Très rare steak	bistecca molto al sangue	Muy raras bistec
Truite	trota	Trucha
Un verre d'. . .	bicchiere di . . .	Un vaso de. . .
Une bouteille d'. . .	bottiglia di . .	Una botella de. . .
Vin blanc	vino bianco	Vino blanco
Vin doux	vino amabile	Vino dulce
Vin rouge	vino rosso	Vino tinto
Vin sec	vino secco	Vino seco
Vinaigre	aceto	Vinagre

French	Italian	Spanish
Well done steak	bistecca ben cotta	Filete bien hecho
Yogourt	yoghurt	Yogur

RESTAURANT
AND BIO STORE LISTINGS
FOR FRANCE
BY REGION

PARIS

Le Citroen davant la Tour Eiffel (R. Levy)

READ THIS FIRST

This section lists 245 Parisian restaurants that serve a gluten-free clientele. It presents these restaurants in several ways:

- alphabetically (see "Restaurants Listed Alphabetically" in the beginning of section).
- by cuisine (see "Cuisine Index" in the beginning of section).
- by *arrondissements* (the numeric French system of identifying neighborhoods) and names of neighborhoods (see "Restaurants Arranged by *Arrondissements*" section).

If you wish to locate **a particular restaurant**, you can use the quick alphabetical list to find its *arrondissement* location. You can then find the extensive information about the restaurant listed with the restaurants organized by *arrondissements*.

If you wish to browse restaurants by **cuisine**, you can look at the quick list "Cuisine Index" and then find the extensive information about each restaurant listed in the "Restaurants listed by *arrondissements/ neighborhoods*" section.

If you wish to browse restaurants by **location**, you can look at the quick list organized by neighborhood/ *arrondissements* and then find the extensive information about each restaurant listed in the "Restaurants listed by *arrondissements/* neighborhoods" section.

The *arrondissements* are arranged by numbers, and correspond, with some overlap, to certain neighborhood names:

NEIGHBORHOODS OF PARIS

1st Arrondissement (Musée Du Louvre/Les Halles)
2nd Arrondissement (La Bourse)
3rd Arrondissement (Le Marais)
4th Arrondissement (Ile De La Cité/Ile St-Louis & Beaubourg)
5th Arrondissement (Latin Quarter)
6th Arrondissement (St-Germain/Luxembourg)
7th Arrondissement (Eiffel Tower/Musée D'orsay)
8th Arrondissement (Champs-Elysées/Madeleine)

9th Arrondissement (Opéra Garnier/Pigalle)
10th Arrondissement (Gare Du Nord/Gare De L'est)
11th & 12th Arrondissements (Opéra Bastille/Bois De Vincennes)
13th Arrondissement (Gobelins/Porte D'ivry)
14th & 15th Arrondissements (Gare Montparnasse/Denfert-Rochereau)
16th Arrondissement (Trocadéro/Bois De Boulogne)
17th Arrondissement (Parc Monceau)
18th Arrondissement (Montmartre)
19th Arrondissement (Buttes Chaumont)
20th Arrondissement (Ménilmontant)

The following information on each venue is provided:
Name   type of venue   cuisine
Address*   phone number** website (if any)
Notes: price point**; reservations, etc.

EXAMPLE:
Des Si & Des Mets   restaurant   bio
63, rue Lepic, 18e.   www.dessietdesmets.com   tel. 01 42 55 19 61
Notes: €€€; highly recommended by celiacs all over the world.

*The *arrondissement* number is provided after the street address. In the
above example, "18e" means that the restaurant is located in the eighteenth
arrondissement.

***Price points are provided when possible (taken from the a la carte menu)
for a main course for 1 incl. 5% tax and service, and are categorized as
follows:

price range	symbol
Under €17	€
€18-€24	€€
€25-€32	€€€
Over €32	€€€€
Not available	N/A

For your convenience we have also listed the major health food stores in
Paris by *arrondissement.*

PARIS RESTAURANTS LISTED ALPHABETICALLY

Use this list to find the arrondissement of a particular restaurant and then look up specific information about the restaurant in the extensive section of restaurants organized by *arrondissements*.

restaurant	arrondissement
7Eme Vin	7
Afghanistan	11
Assiette Aveyronnaise	1
Atelier Aubrac	15
Au Bascou	3
Au Bon Coin	5
Au Bougnat	4
Au Gourmand	1
Au Grain De Folie	18
Au Pere Louis	6
Au Petit Fer À Cheval	4
Au Petit Riche	9
Au Petit Sud Ouest	7
Au Refuge Du Passe	5
Auberge Des Pyrenees Cevennes	11
Auberge Etchégorry	13
Auberge Nicolas Flamel	3
Autour Du Saumon	9
Autour Du Saumon	15
Autour Du Saumon Poisson Paris	4
Aux Ducs De Bourgogne	7
Aux Vieux Paris	4
Babylone	11
Banyan	15
Baratin	20
Bel Canto	4
Bistro Poulbot	18
Bistrot Richelieu	1
Bocconi	8
Bon	16
Boucherie Roulière	5
Breizh Café	3
Buffalo Grill	3

Le Crep'Uscule	18
Le Dome	6
Le Duc	14
Le Framboisy	4
Le Grande Mericourt	11
Le Grenier De Notre-Dame	5
Le Jardin D'En Face	18
Le Jardin D'Ivy	5
Le Machon D'Henri	6
Le Manege De L'Ecuyer	1
Le Manoir	17
Le Melange Des Genres	11
Le Meurice	1
Le Petit Bordelais	7
Le Petit Marché	3
Le Petit Marguery	13
Le Petit Pergolèse	16
Le Petit Pontoise	5
Le Petit Prince De Paris	5
Le Petit Troquet Resturant	7
Le Potager Du Marais	3
Le Pré Catelan	16
Le Reminet	5
Le Restaurant Georges	3
Le Safran Restaurant	8
Le Tagine	11
Le Tastevin	4
Le Temps Des Cerises	13
Le Timbre	6
Le Troquet	15
Le Trumilou	4
Le Vaudeville	2
Le Zéphyr	20
L'Ecailler Du Bistrot	11
L'Enoteca	4
Leo Le Lion	7
Leon De Bruxelles	1
Leon De Bruxelles	4
Leon De Bruxelles	6
Leon De Bruxelles	8

Leon De Bruxelles	9
Leon De Bruxelles	11
Leon De Bruxelles	14
Leon De Bruxelles	17
Les Allobroges	20
Les Degres De Notre Dame	5
Les Deux Palais	4
Les Fables De La Fontaine	7
Les Galopins	11
Les Noces De Jeannette	2
Les Olympiades	5
Les Papilles Bistro	5
Louise Cafe	1
Loving Hut	11
Lui L'Insolent	18
Marguerite	18
Maxim'S	8
Paradis Thai	13
Pasco	14
Petit Bofinger	4
Philou	10
Pierre Gagnaire	8
Pousse-Pousse	9
Prunier	16
Relais Odeon	6
Restaurant De La Tour	15
Restaurant Du Palais Royal	1
Restaurant Le 3	4
Restaurant Mariette	7
Roger La Grenouille	6
Saidoune	17
Savannah Café	5
Saveurs Veget' Halles	1
Senderens	8
Sensing	6
Soya	11
Spoon Food and Wine	8
Taillevent	8
The Greenhouse	11
Tugalik	5

Tugalik	5
Twinkie	2
Un Des Sens	17
Vine et Maree-Voltaire	7
Vine et Maree-Voltaire	11
Vine et Maree-Voltaire	14
Vine et Maree-Voltaire	16
Voy Alimento	10
Wally Le Saharien	9
Willis Wine Bar	1
Yam'Tcha	2
Yugaraj	6
Zimmer Café	1

CUISINE INDEX FOR PARIS RESTAURANTS

<u>arrondissement & name of restaurant</u>   <u>address</u>

AFGHAN
| 11 | **Afghanistan** | 48 rue Saint-Maur |

AMERICAN
3	**Chez Jenny**	39 bd du Temple
9	**Hard Rock Café**	14 boulevard Montmartre
3	**Buffalo Grill**	15 pl de la République
13	**Buffalo Grill**	2 rue Raymond Aron
19	**Buffalo Grill**	29 av Corentin Cariou

ASIAN
| 16 | **Bon** | 25 rue de la Pompe |

BASQUE
| 3 | **Au Bascou** | 38 rue Réaumur |
| 14 | **La Régalade** | 49 av Jean Moulin |

BELGIAN
1	**Leon de Bruxelles**	120 rue Rambuteau
4	**Leon de Bruxelles**	3 bd Beaumarchais
6	**Leon de Bruxelles**	131 bd St-Germain
8	**Leon de Bruxelles**	63 av des Champs-Elysées
9	**Leon de Bruxelles**	8 place de Clichy
11	**Leon de Bruxelles**	8 place de la République
14	**Leon de Bruxelles**	82 bis bd du Montparnasse
17	**Leon de Bruxelles**	95 bd Gouvion-St-Cyr

BIO AND/OR VEGETARIAN
18	**Au Grain de Folie**	24 rue La Vieuville
6	**Guen-maï**	6 rue Cardinale
10	**La Chandelle Verte**	40 rue d'Enghien
5	**Tugalik**	4 rue Toullier
5	**Tugalik**	rue st Placide
3	**Le Potager du Marais**	22 rue Rambuteau
11	**Loving Hut**	92 boulevard Beaumarchais
9	**Pousse-Pousse**	7 rue Notre-Dame-de-Lorette

1	**Saveurs Veget' Halles**	41 rue des bourdonnais
11	**Soya**	20 rue de la Pierre Levée
10	**Voy alimento**	23 rue des Vinaigriers

BISTRO

9	**Au Petit Riche**	25 rue le Peletier
5	**Boucherie Roulière**	24 rue des Canettes
13	**Chez Paul**	22 rue de la Butte aux Cailles
18	**Chez Toinette**	20 rue Germain Pilon
9	**Georgette**	29 rue St-Georges
18	**Just Brigitte plus Elsa (Just B)**	46 rue Caulaincourt
20	**La Boulangerie**	15 rue des Panoyaux
2	**La Bourse ou La Vie**	12 rue Vivienne
19	**La Cave Gourmande**	10 rue du Général Brunet
15	**La Gauloise**	59 av de la Motte-Picquet
16	**La Table Lauriston**	129 rue Lauriston
13	**Le Petit Marguery**	9 bd de Port-Royal
16	**Le Petit Pergolèse**	38 rue Pergolèse
2	**Les Noces de Jeannette**	9 rue d'Amboise
13	**Le Temps des Cerises**	18 rue de la Butte aux Cailles
20	**Le Zéphyr**	1 rue du Jourdain
4	**Petit Bofinger**	6 rue de la Bastille
6	**Roger la Grenouille**	28 rue des Grands Augustins
1	**Zimmer Café**	1 place du Chatelet

BRASSERIE

9	**Charlot - Roi des Coquillages**	12 place de Clichy
8	**La Fermette Marbeuf 1900**	5 rue Marbeuf
5	**La Gueuze**	19 rue Soufflot
4	**Les Deux Palais**	3 Boulevard Palais
8	**senderens**	9 place de la Madelein

BREAKFAST/BRUNCH

| 2 | **Twinkie** | 167 rue Saint-Denis |

CARIBBEAN

| 6 | **Coco & Co.** | 11 rue Bernard Palissy |

CLASSIC FRENCH

| 3 | **Auberge Nicolas Flamel** | 51 rue de Montmorency |

19	Café de la Musique	213 av Jean Jaurès
15	Cave de l'Os à Moëlle	181 rue de Lourmel
8	Dominique Bouchet	11 rue Treilhard
9	La Table d'Anvers	2 place d'Anvers
15	Restaurant de la Tour	6 rue Desaix
7	7eme Vvin	68 av Bosquet
1	Assiette Aveyronnaise	14 rue Coquillière
15	Atelier Aubrac	51 Bld. Garibaldi
5	Au Bon Coin	21 rue de la Collegiale
4	Au Bougnat	26 rue Chanoinesse
6	Au Pere Louis	38 rue Mr Le Prince
4	Au Petit Fer à Cheval	30 rue Vieille du Temple
7	Au Petit Sud Ouest	46 avenue de la Bourdonnais
5	Au Refuge du Passe	32 rue Fer a Moulin
11	Auberge des Pyrenees Cevennes	106 rue de la Folie Mericourt
4	Aux Vieux Paris	24 rue Chanoinesse
20	Baratin	3 rue Jouye-Rouve
4	Bel Canto	72 Quai de l'Hotel de Ville
18	Bistro Poulbot	39 rue Lamarck
1	Bistrot Richelieu	45 rue de Richelieu
3	Breizh Café	109 rue Vieille du Temple
12	Cafe Barge	5 Port de la Rapee
6	Chez Fernand Christine	9 rue Christine
8	Chez Francis	7 place de l'Alma
11	Chez Imogene	25 rue Jean-Pierre Timbaud
11	Chez Paul	13 rue de Charonne
1	Comptoir de la Gastronomie	34 rue Montmartre
4	Equinox	rue des Rosiers
17	Guy Savoy	18 rue Troyon
8	Hilton Arc de Triomphe Paris	51/57 rue de Courcelles
6	La Bastide Odeon	7 rue Corneille
7	La Billebaude	29 rue Exposition
17	La Bonne Heure	11 rue Brochant
1	La Cordonnerie	20 rue St-Roch
1	La Cuisine	14 blvd La Tour-Maubourg
18	La Famille	41 rue des Trois Freres
7	La Petite Chaise	36 rue de Grenelle
4	La Reserve de Quasimodo	4 rue Colombe
1	La Rose de France	24 place Dauphine
18	La Taverne de Montmartre	rue Gabrielle no 25

5	**La Truffiere**	4 rue Blainville
5	**L'agrume**	15 rue des Fosses St-Marcel
5	**L'Aiguiere**	37 rue de Montreuil
13	**L'Aimant du Sud**	40 bd Arago
16	**L'Astrance**	4 rue Beethoven
7	**L'Atelier de Joel Robuchon**	5 rue de Montalembert
15	**L'Atelier du Parc**	35 bd Lefebvre
1	**L'Auberge Café**	4 rue Bertin Poiree
16	**Le Bec Rouge**	46 bd du Montparnasse
17	**Le Bistro du 17eme**	108 Avenue de Villiers
9	**L'Auberge du Clou**	30 av Trudaine
7	**Le Bosquet**	46 avenue Bosquet
8	**le Bristol**	112 rue Faubourg St-Honoré
5	**Le Buisson Ardent**	25 rue Jussieu
7	**Le Clarisse**	29 rue Surcouf
1	**Le Coup d'Etat**	164 rue Saint-Honoré
18	**le crep'uscule**	91 rue Lamarck
4	**Le Framboisy**	16 rue Charlemagne
11	**Le Grande Mericourt**	22 rue de la folie mericourt
18	**Le Jardin d'en Face**	33 rue des trois freres
5	**Le Jardin d'Ivy**	75 rue Mouffetard
6	**Le Machon d'Henri**	8 rue Guisade,
1	**Le Manege De L'ecuyer**	6 rue de la Sourdiere
17	**Le Manoir**	7 rue des Moines
11	**Le Melange des Genres**	44 boulevard Voltaire
7	**Le Petit Bordelais**	22 rue Surcouf
5	**Le Petit Prince de Paris**	12 rue de Lanneau
7	**Le Petit Troquet Resturant**	28 rue Exposition
5	**Le Reminet**	3 rue des Grands-Degres
8	**Le Safran Restaurant**	51/57 rue de Courcelles
11	**Le Tagine**	13 rue Crussol
4	**Le Tastevin**	46 rue Saint-Louis-en-l'Ile
4	**Le Trumilou**	84 Quai de l'hotel de Ville
2	**Le Vaudeville**	29 rue Vivienne
20	**Les Allobroges**	71 rue des Grands-Champs
7	**Leo le Lion**	23 rue Duvivier
11	**Les Galopins**	33 Philippe Auguste
5	**Les Papilles Bistro**	30 rue Gay Lussac
1	**Louise Cafe**	8 rue Croix des Petits Champs
18	**Lui l'insolent**	15 rue Caulaincourt

18	**Marguerite**	50 rue de Clignancourt
10	**Philou**	12 avenue Richerand
7	**Restaurant Mariette**	24 rue Bosquet
8	**Taillevent**	15 rue Lemennais
17	**Un des Sens**	10 rue du Cheroy
9	**Café de la Paix**	12 bd des Capucines
8	**Maxim's**	3 rue Royale
1	**Restaurant du Palais Royal**	110 Galerie de Valois
18	**Des Si & Des Mets Restaurant**	63 rue Lepic

CORSICAN

16	**La Villa Corse**	141, avenue Malakoff
15	**La Villa Corse**	164 bde Grenelle

CREPERIE

7	**Aux Ducs de Bourgogne**	30 rue de Bourgogne

ENGLISH PUB

5	**Le Bombadier Pub**	2 place du Pantheon

FRENCH FUSION

6	**Relais Odeon**	132 boulevard Saint-Germain
4	**Restaurant le 3**	3 rue Sainte-Croix Bretonnerie

GREEK

5	**Les Olympiades**	50 rue Descartes

HAUTE FRENCH

6	**Hélène Darroze**	4 rue d'Assas
6	**Hélène Darroze Salon**	4 rue d'Assas
16	**La Grande Cascade**	Allée de Longchamp
5	**La Tour d'Argent**	15 quai de la Tournelle
8	**Le Cinq**	31 avenue George V
1	**Le Meurice**	228 rue de Rivoli
16	**Le Pré Catelan**	Bois de Boulogne

HEALTHY FAST FOOD

2	**Cojean Bourse**	121 rue Réaumur
16	**Cojean Kléber**	78 avenue Kléber
3	**Cojean Crit**	2 place del la défense

9	**Cojean Figaro**	14 boulevard Haussmann
9	**Cojean Haussmann**	17 boulevard Haussmann
9	**Cojean le Peletier**	30 rue le Peletier
1	**Cojean Louvre**	3 place du Louvre
9	**Cojean Madeleine**	6 rue de Sèze
8	**Cojean Marbeuf**	19 rue Clement Marot
8	**Cojean Mathurins**	64 rue des Mathurins
8	**Cojean Miromesnil**	11 avenue Delcassé
8	**Cojean Monceau**	32 rue Monceau
9	**Cojean Printemps**	64 boulevard Haussmann
9	**Cojean Provence**	66 rue de Provence
1	**Cojean Pyramides**	10 rue des Pyramides
8	**Cojean Roosevelt**	55 ave Franklin Roosevelt
8	**Cojean Washington**	25 rue Washington
13	**EXKi Av de France**	116 Av de France
14	**EXKi Bd Montparnasse**	82 Bd Montparnasse

INDIAN
| 6 | **Yugaraj** | 14, rue Dauphine |

INTERNATIONAL
| 3 | **Le Restaurant Georges** | Centre Pompidou, 6th floor |
| 8 | **Spoon Food and Wine** | 14 rue Marignan |

IRISH
| 11 | **The Greenhouse** | 43 rue Godefroy Cavaignac |

ITALIAN
8	**Bocconi**	10 bis, rue d'Artois 19
17	**da zavola**	11 rue Brochant
1	**Fellini**	58 rue de la Croix Nivert
16	**Giulio Rebellato**	136 rue de la Pompe
7	**Il Sorrentino**	20 rue de Monttessuy
4	**L'Enoteca**	25 rue Charles V

LEBANESE/MIDDLE EASTERN
16	**Fakhr el Dine**	30 rue de Longchamp
17	**Saidoune**	35 rue Legendre
11	**Babylone**	21 rue Daval

MEDITERRANEAN
| 14 | **Pasco** | 74 bd de la Tour Maubourg |
| 5 | **Savannah Café** | 27 rue Descartes |

MEXICAN
| 6 | **Fajitas** | 15 rue Dauphine |
| 4 | **La Perla** | 26 rue Francois Miron |

MODERN FRENCH
1	**Au Gourmand**	17 rue Moliere
7	**Gaya Rive Gauche**	44 rue du Bac
18	**L'Assiette**	78 rue Labat
8	**Pierre Gagnaire**	6 rue Balzac
6	**Sensing**	19 rue Brea
1	**Willis Wine Bar**	13 rue des Petits Champs
3	**Chez Omar**	47 rue de Bretagne

MOROCCAN
| 5 | **Les Degres de Notre Dame** | 10 rue des Grands Degres |

NEW FRENCH
9	**Casa Olympe**	48 rue St-Georges
9	**Jean**	8 rue St-Lazare
13	**L'Avant Goût**	26 rue Bobillot
9	**Le 16 Haussmann**	16 bd Haussmann
3	**Le Petit Marché**	9 rue de Béarn
15	**Le Troquet**	21 rue François Bonvin
2	**yam'tcha**	4 rue Sauval

NORTH AFRICAN
| 9 | **Wally Le Saharien** | 36 rue Rodier |

PROVENCAL
| 3 | **Chez Janou** | 2 rue Roger Verlomme |

SEAFOOD
9	**Autour du Saumon**	56 rue des Martyrs
15	**Autour du Saumon**	116 rue de la Convention
4	**Autour du Saumon Poisson Paris**	60 rue François Miron
6	**Fish la Boissonnerie**	69 rue de Seine

14	**La Cagouille**	10 place Constantin Brancusi
3	**Le Bar à Huîtres**	33 bd Beaumarchais
14	**Le Bistrot du Dôme**	1 rue Delambre
6	**Le Dome**	108 blvd du Montparnasse
14	**Le Duc**	243 bd Raspail
11	**L'Ecailler du Bistrot**	22 rue Paul-Bert
7	**Les Fables de La Fontaine**	131 rue St-Dominique
16	**Prunier**	16 av Victor Hugo
7	**Vine et Maree-Voltaire**	71 avenue de Suffren
11	**Vine et Maree-Voltaire**	276 Boulevard Voltaire
14	**Vine et Maree-Voltaire**	108 Avenue du Maine
16	**Vine et Maree-Voltaire**	183 boulevard Murat

SOUTHWEST FRENCH

13	**Auberge Etchégorry**	41 rue Croulebarbe
15	**Chez Papa**	101 rue de la Croix Nivert
14	**La Cerisaie**	70 bd Edgar Quinet
14	**La Maison Courtine**	157 av du Maine

SWISS, FONDUE

11	**Le Chalet d'Avron**	108 rue de Montreuil

THAI

15	**Banyan**	24 place Etienne Pernet
15	**Erawan**	76 rue de la Fédération
19	**Lao Siam**	49 rue de Belleville
13	**Paradis Thai**	132 rue de Tolbiac

TRADITIONAL FRENCH

6	**La Petite Cour**	8 rue Mabillon
5	**Le Petit Pontoise**	9 rue de Pontoise
6	**Le Timbre**	3 rue Saint Bueve

TUNISIAN

5	**Chez Jaafar**	22 rue Du Sommerard
5	**Le Grenier de Notre-Dame**	18 rue de la Bûcherie

VIETNAMESE

13	**La Bambou Vietnamese**	70 rue Baudricourt

RESTAURANTS LISTED BY ARRONDISSEMENTS
summary of information, with prices

1

Assiette Aveyronnaise	14 rue Coquillière	€
Au Gourmand	17 rue Moliere	€€€€
Bistrot Richelieu	45 rue de Richelieu	€€ - €€€
Comptoir de la Gastronomie	34 rue Montmartre	€€€
Fellini	58 rue de la Croix Nivert	€€€€
La Cordonnerie	20 rue St-Roch	€€
La Cuisine	14 blvd La Tour-Maubourg	€€ - €€€
La Rose de France	24 place Dauphine	€€ - €€€
L'Auberge Café	4 rue Bertin Poiree	€€ - €€€
Le Coup d'Etat	164 rue Saint-Honoré	€€
Le Manege de l'Ecuyer	6 rue de la Sourdiere	€€€ - €€€€
Le Meurice	228 rue de Rivoli-Hotel Meurice	€€€€
Leon de Bruxelles	120 rue Rambuteau	€€€
Louise Cafe	8 rue Croix des Petits Champs	N/A
Restaurant du Palais Royal	110 Galerie de Valois	€€
Saveurs Veget' Halles	41 rue des bourdonnais	€
Willis Wine Bar	13 rue des Petits Champs	€
Zimmer Café	1 place du Chatelet	€€
Cojean Louvre	3 place du Louvre	€
Cojean Pyramides	10 rue des Pyramides	€

2

La Bourse ou La Vie	12 rue Vivienne	€
Le Vaudeville	29 rue Vivienne	€€
Les Noces de Jeannette	9 rue d'Amboise	€€
Twinkie	167 rue Saint-Denis	N/A
yam'tcha	4 rue Sauval .	€€€
Cojean Bourse	121 rue Réaumur	€
EXKi 4 septembre	26 rue du 4 septembre	€
EXKi Bd des Italiens	9 bd des italiens	€

3

Au Bascou	38 rue Réaumur	€€€ - €€€€
Auberge Nicolas Flamel	51 rue de Montmorency	€€€€
Buffalo Grill	15 place de la République	€ - €€
Chez Janou	2 rue Roger Verlomme	N/A
Chez Jenny	39 bd du Temple	€€€€
Chez Omar	47 rue de Bretagne	€€€
Le Bar à Huîtres	33 bd Beaumarchais	€€ - €€€
Le Petit Marché	9 rue de Béarn	€€€ - €€€€
Le Potager du Marais	22 rue Rambuteau	N/A
Le Restaurant Georges	Centre Pompidou, 6th floor	€€€€
Cojean Crit	2 place del la Defense	€
Breizh Café	109 rue Vieille du Temple	€€

4

Au Bougnat	26 rue Chanoinesse	€€ - €€€
Au Petit Fer à Cheval	30 rue Vieille du Temple	€
Autour du Saumon Poisson Paris	60 rue François Miron	€€
Aux Vieux Paris	24 rue Chanoinesse	€€€€
Bel Canto	72 Quai de l'Hotel de Ville	€€€€
Equinox	rue des Rosiers	€€ - €€€
La Perla	26 rue Francois Miron	€€
La Reserve de Quasimodo	4 rue Colombe	€€
Le Framboisy	16 rue Charlemagne	N/A
Le Tastevin	46 rue Saint-Louis-en-l'Ile	€€€€
Le Trumilou	84 quai de l'hotel de ville	€ - €€
L'Enoteca	25 rue Charles V	N/A
Leon de Bruxelles	3 bd Beaumarchais	€€€
Les Deux Palais	3 Boulevard Palais	€ - €€
Petit Bofinger	6 rue de la Bastille	€€
Restaurant le 3	3 rue St-Croix Bretonnerie	€€€ - €€€€

5

Au Bon Coin	21 rue de la Collegiale	€
Au Refuge du Passe	32 rue Fer a Moulin	€€€ - €€€€
Boucherie Roulière	24 rue des Canettes	€€
Chez Jaafar	22 rue Du Sommerard	€-€€€

La Gueuze	19 rue Soufflot	€€
La Tour d'Argent	15 quai de la Tournelle	€€€€
La Truffiere	4 rue Blainville	€€€
L'Agrume	15 rue des Fosses St-Marcel	€€€€
L'Aiguiere	37 rue de Montreuil	€€€€
Le Buisson Ardent	25 rue Jussieu	€€ - €€€
Le Grenier de Notre-Dame	18 rue de la Bûcherie	€ - €€
Le Jardin d'Ivy	75 rue Mouffetard	N/A
Le Petit Prince de Paris	12 rue de Lanneau	€€ - €€€
Le Reminet	3 rue des Grands-Degres	N/A
Les degres de notre dame	10 rue des Grands Degres	€€
Les Olympiades	50 rue Descartes	€
Savannah Café	27 rue Descartes	€
Tugalik	4 rue Toullier	€€
Tugalik	rue St Placide	€€
Le Bombadier Pub	2 place du Pantheon	€
Les Papilles Bistro	30 rue Gay Lussac	N/A
Le Petit Pontoise	9 rue de Pontoise	€€

6

Au Pere Louis	38 rue Mr LE Prince	€€
Chez Fernand Christine	9 rue Christine	€€€ - €€€€
Coco & Co.	11 rue Bernard Palissy	N/A
Fajitas	15 rue Dauphine	N/A
Fish la Boissonnerie	69 rue de Seine	€€€€
Guen-maï	6 rue Cardinale	€ - €€
Hélène Darroze	4 rue d'Assas	€€€€
La Bastide Odeon	7 rue Corneille	€€€€
La Petite Cour	8, rue Mabillon	€€€ - €€€€
Le Dome	108 blvd du Montparnasse	€€€€
Le Machon d'Henri	8 rue Guisade	N/A
Le Timbre	3 rue Saint Bueve	€€€
Leon de Bruxelles	131 bd St-Germain	€€€
Relais Odeon	132 Boulevard Saint-Germain	€€€
Roger la Grenouille	28 rue des Grands Augustins	€€€€
Sensing	19 rue Brea	€€€€
Yugaraj	14 rue Dauphine	€€
Hélène Darroze	4 rue d'Assas	€€€€

7

7eme Vin	68 av Bosquet	€€€ - €€€€
Au Petit Sud Ouest	46 avenue de la Bourdonna	N/A
Gaya Rive Gauche	44 rue du Bac	€€€€
Il Sorrentino	20 rue de Monttessuy	€€
La Billebaude	29 rue Exposition	N/A
La Petite Chaise	36 rue de Grenelle	€€
L'Atelier de Joel Robuchon	5 rue de Montalembert	€€€€
Le Bosquet	46 Avenue Bosquet	€€
Le Clarisse	29 rue Surcouf	€€€€
Le Petit Bordelais	22 rue Surcouf	€€€ - €€€€
Le Petit Troquet Resturant	28 rue Exposition	€€€ - €€€€
Leo le Lion	23 rue Duvivier	€€
Les Fables de La Fontaine	131 rue St-Dominique	€€€€
Restaurant Mariette	24 rue Bbosquet	€ - €€
Vine et Maree-Voltaire	71 avenue de Suffren	€€€€

8

Bocconi	10 bis, rue d'Artois	€€€€
Chez Francis	7 place de l'Alma	€€€
Dominique Bouchet	11 rue Treilhard	€€€€
Le Bristol	112 rue Faubourg Saint-Honoré	€€€€
Le Cinq	31 Avenue George V	€€€€
Le Safran Restaurant	51/57 rue de Courcelles	€€€€
Leon de Bruxelles	63 av des Champs-Elysées	€€€
Maxim's	3 rue Royale	€€€€
Pierre Gagnaire	6 rue Balzac	€€€€
Senderens	9 place de la Madelein	€€€€
Spoon Food and Wine	14 rue Marignan	€€€€
Taillevent	15 rue Lemennais, 8E	€€€€
Hilton Arc de Triomphe Paris	51/57 rue de Courcelles	€€€€
Cojean Marbeuf	19 rue Clement Marot	€
Cojean Mathurins	64 rue des Mathurins	€
Cojean Miromesnil	11 avenue Déclassé	€
Cojean Monceau	32 rue Monceau	€
Cojean Roosevelt	55 ave Franklin Delano Roosevelt	€
Cojean Washington	25 rue Washington	€
La Fermette Marbeuf 1900	5 rue Marbeuf	€€€

9

Au Petit Riche	25 rue le Peletier	€€€€
Autour du Saumon	56 rue des Martyrs	€€
Café de la Paix	12 bd des Capucines	€€€€
Casa Olympe	48 rue St-Georges	€€€€
Charlot - Roi des Coquillages	12 place de Clichy	€€€
Georgette	29 rue St-Georges	€€€€
Hard Rock Café	14 Boulevard Montmartre	N/A
Jean	8 rue St-Lazare	€€€€
La Table d'Anvers	2 place d'Anvers	€€
L'Auberge du Clou	30 av Trudaine	€€€ - €€€€
Le 16 Haussmann	16 bd Haussmann	€€€€
Leon de Bruxelles	8 place de Clichy	€€€
Pousse-Pousse	7 rue Notre-Dame-de-Lorette	€ - €€
Wally Le Saharien	36 rue Rodier	€€€€
Cojean Figaro	14 boulevard Haussmann	€
Cojean Haussmann	17 boulevard Haussmann	€
Cojean le Peletier	30 rue le Peletier	€
Cojean Madeleine	6 rue de Sèze	€
Cojean Printemps	64 boulevard Haussmann	€
Cojean Provence	66 rue de Provence	€

10

La Chandelle Verte	40 rue d'Enghien	€ - €€
Philou	12 avenue Richerand	€€€
Voy Alimento	23 rue des Vinaigriers	€ - €€

11

Afghanistan	48 rue Saint-Maur	€
Auberge des Pyrenees Cevennes	106 rue Folie Mericourt	€€€ - €€€€
Babylone	21 rue Daval	€€
Chez Imogene	25 rue Jean-Pierre Timbaud	€
Chez Paul	13 rue de Charonne	€€€€
Le Chalet d'Avron	108 rue de Montreuil	€
Le Grande Mericourt	22 rue de la Folie mericourt	€€€ - €€€€
Le Melange des Genres	44 boulevard Voltaire	€ - €€
Le Tagine	13 rue Crussol	€€€

L'Ecailler du Bistrot	22 rue Paul-Bert	€€ - €€€
Leon de Bruxelles	8 place de la République	€€€
Les Galopins	33 Philippe Auguste	€€ - €€€
Loving Hut	92 boulevard Beaumarchais	€
Soya	20 rue de la Pierre Levée	€
The Greenhouse	43 rue Godefroy Cavaignac	€
Vine et Maree-Voltaire	276 boulevard Voltaire	€€€€

12

Cafe Barge	5 Port de la Rapee	€€ - €€€

13

Auberge Etchégorry	41 rue Croulebarbe	€€€
Buffalo Grill	2 rue Raymond Aron	€ - €€
Chez Paul	22 rue de la Butte aux Cailles	€€€€
La Bambou Vietnamese	70 rue Baudricourt	€€
Paradis Thai	132 rue de Tolbiac	N/A
L'Aimant du Sud	40 bd Arago	€€
L'Avant Goût	26 rue Bobillot	€€€
Le Petit Marguery	9 bd de Port-Royal	€€€€
Le Temps des Cerises	18 rue de la Butte aux Cailles	€€
EXKi Av de France	116 Av de France	€

14

La Cagouille	10 pl Constantin Brancusi	€€€€
La Cerisaie	70 bd Edgar Quinet	€€
La Maison Courtine	157 av du Maine	€€€ - €€€€
La Régalade	49 av Jean Moulin	€€€€
Le Bistrot du Dôme	1 rue Delambre	€€
Le Duc	243 bd Raspail	€€€€
Leon de Bruxelles	82 bis bd du Montparnasse	€€€
Pasco	74 bd de la Tour Maubourg	€€€
Vine et Maree-Voltaire	108 avenue du Maine	€€€€

15

Atelier Aubrac	51 bld. Garibaldi	€
Autour du Saumon	116 rue de la Convention	€€ - €€€

Banyan	24 pl Etienne Pernet	€€€ - €€€€
Cave de l'Os à Moëlle	181 rue de Lourmel	€€€€
Chez Papa	101 rue de la Croix Nivert	€ - €€
Erawan	76 rue de la Fédération	€€€€
La Gauloise	59 av de la Motte-Picquet	€€€€
L'Atelier du Parc	35 Bd Lefebvre	€€
Le Troquet	21 rue François Bonvin	€€€€
La Villa Corse	164 bd de Grenelle	€€€ - €€€€
Restaurant de la Tour	6 rue Desaix	€€ - €€€

16

Bon	25 rue de la Pompe	€€€
Fakhr el Dine	30 rue de Longchamp	€€€€
Giulio Rebellato	136 rue de la Pompe	€€€ - €€€€
L'Astrance	4 rue Beethoven	€€€
La Grande Cascade	Allée de Longchamp	€€€€
La Table Lauriston	129 rue Lauriston	€€€€
La Villa Corse	141 avenue Malakoff	€€€ - €€€€
Le Bec Rouge	46 bd du Montparnasse	€€€€
Le Petit Pergolèse	38 rue Pergolèse	€€€€
Le Pré Catelan	Bois de Boulogne, Route Suresnes	€€€€
Prunier	16 av Victor Hugo	€€€€
Vine et Maree-Voltaire	183 boulevard Murat	€€€€
Cojean Kléber	78 avenue Kléber	€

17

Da Zavola	11 rue Brochant	N/A
Guy Savoy	18 rue Troyon	€€€€
La Bonne Heure	11 rue Brochant	€
Le Bistro du 17eme	108 Avenue de Villiers	€€€ - €€€€
Le Manoir	7 rue des Moines	€
Leon de Bruxelles	95 bd Gouvion-St-Cyr	€€€
Saidoune	35 rue Legendre	€ - €€
Un des Sens	10 rue du Cheroy	N/A

18

Au Grain de Folie	24 rue La Vieuville	€
Bistro Poulbot	39 rue Lamarck	€€
Chez Toinette	20 rue Germain Pilon	€€
Des Si & Des Mets Restaurant	63 rue Lepic	€€
La Famille	41 rue des Trois Frères	€€
La Taverne de Montmartre	rue Gabrielle no 25	€€ - €€€
L'Assiette	78 rue Labat	€€€
Le Crep'Uscule	91 rue Lamarck	€€€
Le Jardin d'en Face	33 rue des trois frères	€€ - €€€
Lui l'Insolent	15 rue Caulaincourt	€€
Marguerite	50 rue de Clignancourt	€€ - €€€

19

Buffalo Grill	29 av Corentin Cariou	€ - €€
Café de la Musique	213 av Jean Jaurès	N/A
Chez Vincent	Parc des Buttes Chaumont	€€€
La Cave Gourmande	10 rue du Général Brunet	€€€€
Lao Siam	49 rue de Belleville	€€€ - €€€€

20

Baratin	3 rue Jouye-Rouve	€€€ - €€€€
La Boulangerie	15 rue des Panoyaux	€€€ - €€€€
Les Allobroges	71 rue des Grands-Champs	€€€€
Le Zéphyr	1 rue du Jourdain	€€

HEALTH FOOD STORES
LISTED BY ARRONDISSEMENTS

1
La Vie Claire   76-80 rue Saint Honore

3
Biocoop Lemo Sebastopol   66 boulevard De Sébastopol
Bio-Moi   35 rue Debelleyme

4
Naturalia   11 rue Renard
Naturalia Saint-Antoine   59 rue Saint-Antoine

5
La Vie Claire   79 rue Claude Bernard
Naturalia Monge   36 rue Monge

6
Naturalia Raspail   116 boulevard Raspail

7
Naturalia La Motte Picquet   38 avenue De La Motte Picquet

8
La Vie Claire   85 boulevard Haussman
Naturalia   21 bd Des Batignolles

9
Biocoop Du Faubourg   73 rue Du Faubourg Poissonnière
Naturalia   43 bd De Clichy
Naturalia Lamartine   37 rue Lamartine

10
La Vie Claire   9 /11 Place Du Colonel Fabien
Naturalia Beaurepaire   24 rue Beaurepaire
Naturalia Magenta   73 boulevard Magenta
Naturalis Beaurepaire   24 rue Beaurepaire

11

Biocoop Le Retour A La Terre	114 avenue Philippe Auguste
Biocoop Lemo	33 boulevard Voltaire
Biosphare	57 rue Saint Maur
La Vie Claire	42 boulevard Du Temple
La Vie Claire	255 boulevard Voltaire
Naturalia	33 rue de La Roquette
Naturalia	119 rue de Montreuil
Naturalia Richard Lenoir	108 bd Richard Lenoir
Naturalia Voltaire	196 bd Voltaire

12

Biocoop Paris 12ème	47 rue Jacques Hillairet
Naturalia Bizot	72-74 Avenue Général Michel Bizot

13

Biocoop Paris Glaciere	55 rue De La Glacière
Naturalia	44 Av Italie
Naturalia Tolbiac	71 rue De Tolbiac

14

Bio Paris Catalogne	2 place de Catalogne
L'Elan Nature	107 Bis rue Gen Leclerc
Naturalia Brezin	13 rue Brézin

15

Biocoop Grenelle	44 bd De Grenelle
La Vie Claire	20 rue De L'eglise
La Vie Claire	60 rue Brancion
Naturalia	332 rue Lecourbe
Naturalia Cambronne	86 rue de Cambronne
Naturalia Convention	222 rue de La Convention

16

La Vie Claire	25 rue de L'annonciation
Naturalia Sablons	25 rue des Sablons

17

Biocoop Paris	153 rue Legendre
Naturalia	107 Bis av de St Ouen

Naturalia Bayen	11 rue Bayen
Naturalia Bayen	11 rue Bayen
Naturalia Levis	16 rue Levis

18
Naturalia	37 rue du Poteau
Naturalia	41 rue Lepic
Naturalia	118 rue Caulaincourt

19
| **Canal Bio** | 46 Bis Quai De La Loire |
| **Naturalia Meaux** | 59 rue De Meaux |

20
Biocoop Belleville En Bio	62 rue De Belleville
La Vie Claire	13 Bis, Avenue Du Père Lachaise
La Vie Claire	305 rue Des Pyrenees
Naturalia Jourdain	2 rue Du Jourdain
Naturalia Pyrenees	180 Bis rue Des Pyrénées

Rodin's "Thinker"; Rodin Museum (J. Clayton)

PARIS RESTAURANTS AND HEALTH FOOD STORES LISTED BY ARRONDISSEMENT

1ER ARRONDISSEMENT

Assiette Aveyronnaise restaurant   French
14 rue Coquillière, 1er. tel. 01 42 36 51 60
http://www.aveyron.com/english/phbistro/AssietteUK.html
Notes: €. "Just come."

Au Gourmand restaurant Modern French
17 rue Moliere, 1er. tel. 01 42 96 22 19
www.restaurantaugourmandparis.com
Notes: €€€€

Bistrot Richelieu restaurant   French
45 rue de Richelieu, 1er. tel. 01 42 60 19 16 bistrotrichelieu.fr
Notes: €€ - €€€. No need for advance notice.

Comptoir de la Gastronomie restaurant French
34 rue Montmartre, 1er. tel. 01 42 33 31 32 comptoir-gastronomie.com
Notes: €€€. Advance notice necessary.

Fellini restaurant   Italian
58 rue de la Croix Nivert, 1er. tel. 01 45 77 40 77
Notes: €€€€. Average dinner for one €54.

La Cordonnerie restaurant   French
20 rue St-Roch, 1er. tel. 01 42 60 17 42
www.restaurantlacordonnerie.com
Notes: €€. Very accommodating. Advance notice necessary.

La Cuisine restaurant   French
14 boulevard La Tour-Maubourg, 1er. tel. 01 44 18 36 32
lacuisine.lesrestos.com
Notes: €€ - €€€. Call ahead. In the Palais neighborhood.

La Rose de France restaurant   French
24 place Dauphine, 1er. tel. 01 43 54 10 12 www.larosedefrance.com
Notes: €€ - €€€

L'Auberge Café   restaurant   French
4 rue Bertin Poiree, 1er.   tel. 01 43 29 01 22
Notes: €€ - €€€. Advance notice necessary.

Le Coup d'Etat   restaurant   French
164 rue Saint-Honoré, 1er.   tel. 01 42 60 27 66
Notes: €€

Le Manege De L'ecuyer   restaurant   French
6 rue de la Sourdiere, 1er.   tel. 01 49 27 00 64
Notes: €€€ - €€€€. "No problem". English spoken. Advance notice
necessary.

Le Meurice   restaurant   haute French
228 rue de Rivoli-Hotel Meurice, 1er.   tel. 01 44 58 10 50
www.meuricehotel.com
Notes: €€€€

Leon de Bruxelles   restaurant   Belgian
120 rue Rambuteau, 1er.   tel. 01 42 36 18 50
www.leon-de-bruxelles.fr
Notes: €€€. This restaurant is part of a large chain all over France. They have
limited items that are GF, but their Director of Quality Control nationwide
provided us with a list of menu items that are GF.

Louise Cafe   restaurant   French
8 rue Croix des Petits Champs, 1er.   tel. 01 42 60 22 44
Notes: N/A. Some plates can be made GF.

Restaurant du Palais Royal   restaurant   French Classic
110 Galerie de Valois, 1er.   tel. 01 40 20 00 27
www.restaurantdupalaisroyal.com/
Notes: €€

Saveurs Veget' Halles   restaurant   vegetarian
41 rue des Bourdonnais, 1er.   tel. 01 40 41 93 95
www.saveursvegethalles.fr
Notes: €. GF items are indicated on menu

Willis Wine Bar   restaurant   Modern French
13 rue des Petits Champs, 1er.   tel. 01 42 61 05 09
www.williswinebar.com
Notes: €

Zimmer Café   restaurant   bistro
1 place du Chatelet, 1er.   tel. 01 42 36 74 03   www.lezimmer.com
Notes: €€

La Vie Claire   health food store   76-80 rue Saint Honore, 1er.

Cojean louvre   Fast, healthy food   GF soups and salads
3 place du Louvre, 1er.   tel. 01 40 13 06 80   www.cojean.fr
Notes: €. Open Monday-Friday 10-4

Cojean pyramides   Fast, healthy food   GF soups and salads
10 rue des Pyramides, 1er.   tel. 01 42 96 00 50   www.cojean.fr
Notes: €. Open Monday-Saturday 10-4

2^E ARRONDISSEMENT

La Bourse ou La Vie   restaurant   bistro
12 rue Vivienne, 2e.   tel. 01 42 60 08 83
Notes: €. Very limited menu.

le vaudeville   restaurant   French
29 rue Vivienne, 2e.   tel. 01 43 26 25 70 www.vaudevilleparis.com
Notes: €€

Les Noces de Jeannette restaurant   bistro
9 rue d'Amboise, 2e. tel. 01 42 96 36 89   www.lesnocesdejeannette.com
Notes: €€. Advance notice necessary.

Twinkie   restaurant   breakfast/brunch
167 rue Saint-Denis, 2e.   tel. 01 42 36 92 58
www.twinkie-breakfasts.com
Notes: N/A. Has a number of GF and DF items.

yam'tcha   restaurant   New French
4 rue Sauval, 2e.   tel. 01 40 26 08 07
Notes: €€€

Cojean bourse   Fast, healthy food   French
121 rue Réaumur, 2e.   tel. 01 42 36 58 11   www.cojean.fr
Notes: €. Open Monday-Friday 10-4

EXKi 4 septembre   Fast, healthy food
26 rue du 4 septembre, 2e.   www.exki.fr
Notes: €. Some dishes have been labeled "SF" or "sans gluten"

EXKi Bd des italiens   Fast, healthy food
9 bd des Italiens, 2e.   www.exki.fr
Notes: €. Some dishes have been labeled "SF" or "sans gluten"

3^E ARRONDISSEMENT

Au Bascou   restaurant   basque
38 rue Réaumur, 3e.   tel. 01 42 72 69 24   www.au-bascou.fr
Notes: €€€ - €€€€. Very nice staff. "Just come." "Of course!"

Auberge Nicolas Flamel restaurant   Classic French
51 rue de Montmorency, 3e.   tel. 01 42 71 77 78
www.auberge-nicolas-flamel.fr
Notes: €€€€. Mention GF when you make reservations.average dinner for
one €54.

Buffalo Grill   restaurant   American steakhouse
15 pl de la République, 3e.   tel. 01 40 29 94 98   www.buffalo-grill.fr
Notes: € - €€. This restaurant chain has a list of dishes which are gluten-free.

Chez Janou   restaurant   Provence
2 rue Roger Verlomme, 3e.   tel. 01 42 72 28 41   www.chezjanou.com
Notes: N/A

Chez Jenny   restaurant   Alsace brasserie
39 bd du Temple, 3e.   tel. 01 44 54 39 00   www.chezjenny.com
Notes: €€€€. Please give one day advance notice for GF.

Chez Omar   restaurant   Moroccan
47 rue de Bretagne, 3e.   tel. 01 42 72 36 26
Notes: €€€. average dinner for one €32.

Le Bar à Huîtres   restaurant   Seafood
33 bd Beaumarchais, 3e.   tel. 01 48 87 98 92   www.lebarahuitres.fr
Notes: €€ - €€€. Reservations necessary but you can announce GF needs
when you come.

Le Petit Marché   restaurant   New French
9 rue de Béarn, 3e.   tel. 01 42 72 06 67
Notes: €€€ - €€€€

Le Potager du Marais restaurant   bio/vegetarian
22 rue Rambuteau, 3e.   tel. 01 42 74 24 66 www.lepotagerdumarais.com
Notes: N/A

Le Restaurant Georges   restaurant   International
Centre Pompidou 6th floor, 3e.   tel. 01 44 78 47 99
www.centrepompidou.fr
Notes: €€€€. main entrées €37-€47.

Biocoop Lemo Sebastopol   health food store
66 boulevard de Sébastopol, 3e.

Bio-Moi   health food store   35 rue Debelleyme, 3e.

Cojean crit   Fast, healthy food   GF soups and salads
2 place del la Défense, 3e.   tel. 01 40 81 08 13   www.cojean.fr
Notes: €. Open Monday-Friday 10-5

Breizh Café   Café/crêperie   French
109 rue Vieille du Temple, 3e.   tel. 01 42 72 13 77
www.breizhcafe.com/fr-breizh-cafe-paris-acce.html
Notes: €€

4^E ARRONDISSEMENT

Au Bougnat   restaurant   French
26 rue Chanoinesse, 4e.   tel. 01 43 54 50 74
Notes: €€ - €€€. No advance notice necessary.

Au Petit Fer à Cheval   restaurant   French
30 rue Vieille du Temple, 4e.   tel. 01 42 72 47 47   www.cafeine.com
Notes: €

Autour du Saumon Poisson Paris   restaurant   Seafood
60 rue François Miron, 4e.   tel. 01 42 77 23 08   http://autourdusaumon.eu
Notes: €€. English spoken.

Aux Vieux Paris   restaurant   French
24 rue Chanoinesse, 4e.   tel. 01 10 51 78 52   www.auvieuxparis.fr
Notes: €€€€

Bel Canto   restaurant   French
72 Quai de l'Hotel de Ville, 4e.   tel. 01 42 78 30 18   www.lebelcanto.com
Notes: €€€€

Equinox   restaurant   French
rue des Rosiers, 4e.   tel. 01 40 41 95 03
Notes: €€ - €€€

La Perla   restaurant   Mexican
26 rue Francois Miron, 4e.   tel. 01 42 77 59 40
Notes: €€. "Just come."

La reserve de quasimodo restaurant   French
4 rue Colombe, 4e.   tel. 01 46 34 67 67
Notes: €€

Le Framboisy   restaurant   French
16 rue Charlemagne, 4e.   tel. 01 42 72 14 16   www.leframboisy.com
Notes: N/A

Le Tastevin   restaurant   French
46 rue Saint-Louis-en-l'Ile, 4e.   tel. 01 43 54 17 31
www.letastevin-paris.com/index.html
Notes: €€€€. No problem. Advance notice.

le trumilou   restaurant   French
84 quai de l'hotel de Ville, 4e.   tel. 01 42 77 63 98   www.letrumilou.fr
Notes: € - €€

L'Enoteca   restaurant   Italian
25 rue Charles V, 4e.   tel. 01 42 78 91 44   www.enocateca.fr
Notes: N/A

Leon de Bruxelles   restaurant   Belgian
3 bd Beaumarchais, 4e.   tel. 01 42 71 75 55   www.leon-de-bruxelles.fr
Notes: €€€. This restaurant is part of a large chain all over France. They have
limited items that are GF, but their Director of Quality Control nationwide
provided us with a list of menu items that are GF.

Les Deux Palais   restaurant   brasserie
3 boulevard Palais, 4e.   tel. 01 43 54 20 86
Notes: € - €€

Petit Bofinger   restaurant   bistro
6 rue de la Bastille, 4e.   tel. 01 42 72 05 23 http://www.flobrasseries.com/
Notes: €€. Advance notice necessary. Many celiac clients.

Restaurant le 3   restaurant   fusion
3 rue Sainte-Croix de la Bretonnerie 75004, 4e.   tel. 01 42 74 71 52
www.letrois.com
Notes: €€€ - €€€€

Fountain in front of Centre Pompidou (J.Clayton)

Naturalia   health food store   11 rue Renard, 4e.
Naturalia Saint-Antoine health food store   59 rue Saint-Antoine, 4e.

5^E ARRONDISSEMENT

Au Bon Coin   restaurant   French
21 rue de la Collegiale, 5e.   tel. 01 43 31 55 57   www.auboncoin-
restaurant.com
Notes: €. Many celiac clients. Many plates can be made GF. The staff goes
out of their way for you.

Au Refuge du Passe   restaurant   French
32 rue Fer a Moulin, 5e.   tel. 01 47 07 29 91
Notes: €€€ - €€€€. "No problem."

Boucherie Roulière   restaurant   Bistro
24 rue des Canettes, 5e.   tel. 01 43 26 25 70
Notes: €€

Chez Jaafar   restaurant   Tunisian
22 rue du Sommerard, 5e.   tel. 01 46 33 95 40 www.restaurantjaafar.com
Notes: €-€€€. Do not order dishes with couscous.

La Gueuze   restaurant   Brasserie
19 rue Soufflot, 5e.   tel. 01 43 54 63 00   http://www.la-gueuze.com
Notes: €€

La Tour d'Argent   restaurant   Haute French
15 quai de la Tournelle, 5e. tel. 01 43 54 23 31   www.latourdargent.com
Notes: €€€€. Reservations essential. Jacket and tie at dinner.

La Truffiere   restaurant   French
4 rue Blainville, 5e.   tel. 01 46 33 29 82   www.la-truffiere.fr/
Notes: €€€. Advance notice necessary. In the pantheon neighborhood.

L'agrume   restaurant   French
15 rue des Fosses St-Marcel, 5e. tel. 01 43 31 86 48
Notes: €€€€. "Yes absolutely." Call ahead for reservations because the restaurant gets very crowded.

L'Aiguiere   restaurant   French
37 rue de Montreuil, 5e. tel. 01 43 72 42 32
Notes: €€€€. Advance notice necessary. In the Popincourt district.

Le Buisson Ardent   restaurant   French
25 rue Jussieu, 5e.   tel. 01 43 54 93 02
Notes: €€ - €€€. In the pantheon district. Many celiac clients. "Avec plaisir".

Le Grenier de Notre-Dame restaurant   vegetarian
18 rue de la Bûcherie, 5e. tel. 01 43 29 98 29
Notes: € - €€. Reservations recommended.

Le Jardin d'Ivy   restaurant   French
75 rue Mouffetard, 5e. tel. 01 47 07 19 29 www.lejardindivy.com
Notes: N/A

Le Petit Prince de Paris restaurant   French
12 rue de Lanneau, 5e. tel. 01 43 54 77 26 www.lepetitprincedeparis.com
Notes: €€ - €€€. In the pantheon district. "Of course". Advance notice necessary.

Le Reminet   restaurant   French
3 rue des Grands-Degres, 5e. tel. 01 44 07 04 24 http://www.lereminet.com/

Les Degres De Notre Dame restaurant   Moroccan
10 rue des Grands Degres, 5e. tel. 01 55 42 88 88 www.lesdegreshotel.com
Notes: €€

Les Olympiades restaurant Greek
50 rue Descartes, 5e. tel. 01 43 54 28 47
Notes: €. In the pantheon district.

Savannah Café restaurant Mediterranean
27 rue Descartes, 5e. tel. 01 43 29 45 77 www.savannahcafe.fr/
Notes: €. "Yes, of course!" English spoken. In the pantheon neighborhood.

Tugalik restaurant bio
4 rue Toullier (bet. Sorbonne & Luxembourg), 5e. tel. 01 43 54 41 49
http://www.tugalik.com/
Notes: €€

Tugalik restaurant bio
rue st Placide (bet. rue de Rennes & le Bon marché), 5e. tel. 01 43 54 41 49
http://www.tugalik.com/
Notes: €€

Le Bombadier Pub Pub British style English pub
2 place du Pantheon, 5e. tel. 01 43 54 79 22
Notes: €

Les Papilles Bistro Deli/restaurant/wine cellar French
30 rue Gay Lussac, 5e. tel. 01 43 25 20 79 www.lespapillesparis.com
Notes: N/A. Owner very helpful and speaks perfect English.

Le Petit Pontoise bistro Traditional French
9 rue de Pontoise, 5e. tel. 01 43 29 25 20 www.petitpontoise.com
Notes: €€

La Vie Claire health food store 79 rue Claude Bernard, 5e.
Naturalia Monge health food store 36 rue Monge, 5e.

6ᴱ ARRONDISSEMENT

Hélène Darroze salon restaurant haute French
4 rue d'Assas, 6e. tel. 01 42 22 00 11
http://www.helenedarroze.com/en/restaurant
Notes: €€€€. Fixed-price dinners €88.

Au Pere Louis restaurant French
38 rue Mr LE Prince, 6e. tel. 01 43 26 54 14
Notes: €€

Chez Fernand Christine restaurant   French
9 rue Christine, 6e.   tel. 01 43 54 61 47
Notes: €€€ - €€€€

Coco & Co.   restaurant   Caribbean
11 rue Bernard Palissy, 6e.   tel. 01 45 44 02 52   www.cocoandco.fr
Notes: N/A. English spoken. "With pleasure" . Explain your dietary needs
when you get there.average dinner for one €16.

Fajitas   restaurant   Mexican
15 rue Dauphine, 6e.   tel. 01 46 34 44 69   www.fajitas-paris.com
Notes: N/A

Notre Dame (J.Clayton)

Fish la Boissonnerie   restaurant   Seafood
69 rue de Seine, 6e.   tel. 01 43 54 34 69
Notes: €€€€. Call ahead and tell them what you can and can't eat.

Guen-maï   restaurant   bio
6 rue Cardinale, 6e.   tel. 01 43 26 03 24
Notes: € - €€. "Just come."

Hélène Darroze   restaurant   haute French
4 rue d'Assas, 6e.   tel. 01 42 22 00 11   www.helenedarroze.com
Notes: €€€€. Main courses €48-€72.

La Bastide Odeon   restaurant   French
7 rue Corneille, 6e.   tel. 01 43 26 03 65   www.bastide-odeon.com
Notes: €€€€. Luxembourg neighborhood. Average dinner for one €55

La Petite Cour   restaurant   traditional French
8 rue Mabillon, 6e.   tel. 01 43 26 52 26   www.lapetitecour.fr
Notes: €€€ - €€€€. Luxembourg neighborhood.

Le Dome   restaurant   seafood
108 boulevard du Montparnasse, 6e.   tel. 01 43 35 25 81
Notes: €€€€. Any time. A lot of things can be made gluten-free. Need for
reservations. "You must come when you're in Paris."

Le Machon d'Henri   restaurant   French
8 rue Guisade, 6e.   tel. 01 43 29 08 70
Notes: N/A. No advance notice necessary.

Le Timbre   restaurant   Traditional French
3 rue Saint Bueve, 6e.   tel. 01 45 49 10 40 www.restaurantletimbre.com
Notes: €€€

Leon de Bruxelles   restaurant   Belgian
131 bd St-Germain, 6e.   tel. 01 43 26 45 95   www.leon-de-bruxelles.fr
Notes: €€€. This restaurant is part of a large chain all over France. They have
limited items that are GF, but their Director of Quality Control nationwide
provided us with a list of menu items that are GF. See page 16.

Relais Odeon   restaurant   fusion
132 boulevard Saint-Germain, 6e.   tel. 01 43 29 81 80
www.relaisodeon.com/
Notes: €€€. "Of course, no problem. "Just come."" In the Luxembourg
neighborhood.

Roger la Grenouille   restaurant   bistro
28 rue des Grands Augustins, 6e.   tel. 01 56 24 24 34
Notes: €€€€. Luxembourg neighborhood.

Sensing   restaurant   Modern French
19 rue Brea, 6e.   tel. 01 43 27 08 80   www.restaurantsensing.com
Notes: €€€€. Advance notice necessary. In the Luxembourg neighborhood

Yugaraj   restaurant   Indian
14 rue Dauphine, 6e.   tel. 01 43 26 44 91   www.yugaraj.com
Notes: €€. Main entrées €20-€32.

Naturalia Raspail   health food store
116 boulevard Raspail, 6e.

7^E ARRONDISSEMENT

7eme vin   restaurant   French
68 av Bosquet, 7e.   tel. 01 45 51 15 97   www.septiemevin.fr
Notes: €€€ - €€€€. Advance reservations suggested.

Au Petit Sud Ouest   restaurant   French
46 avenue de la Bourdonnais, 7e.   tel. 01 45 55 59 59
www.au-petit-sud-ouest.fr
Notes: N/A. Advance notice necessary.

Gaya Rive Gauche   restaurant   Modern French
44 rue du Bac, 7e.   tel. 01 45 44 73 73   www.pierregagnaire.com
Notes: €€€€. Reservations necessary.average dinner for one €79.

Il Sorrentino   restaurant   Italian
20 rue de Monttessuy, 7e.   tel. 01 45 55 12 50
Notes: €€. Many things can be made gluten-free.

La Billebaude   restaurant   French
29 rue Exposition, 7e.   tel. 01 45 55 20 96
Notes: N/A. Advance reservations recommended.

La Petite Chaise   restaurant   French
36rue de Grenelle, 7e.   tel. 01 42 22 13 35 www.alapetitechaise.fr/
Notes: €€. No advance reservations necessary. In the Palais neighborhood.

Statue (L.Schulz)

L'Atelier de Joel Robuchon   restaurant   French
5 rue de Montalembert, 7e.   tel. 01 42 22 56 56
www.joel-robuchon.com
Notes: €€€€. Reservations necessary.

Le Bosquet   restaurant   French
46 avenue Bosquet, 7e.   tel. 01 45 51 38 13 www.bosquetparis.com
Notes: €€. Reservations needed only for parties of five or more.

Le Clarisse   restaurant   French
29 rue Surcouf, 7e.   tel. 01 45 50 11 10   www.leclarisse.fr
Notes: €€€€. Advance notice preferable.

Le Petit Bordelais   restaurant   French
22 rue Surcouf, 7e. tel. 01 45 51 46 93   http://www.le-petit-bordelais.fr
Notes: €€€ - €€€€. Advance reservations.

Le Petit Troquet Resturant restaurant   French
28 rue Exposition, 7e.   tel. 01 47 05 80 39
http://restaurant.abemadi.com/e/74.html
Notes: €€€ - €€€€

Leo le Lion   restaurant   French
23 rue Duvivier, 7e.   tel. 01 45 51 41 77 http://leo.le.lion.voila.net/
Notes: €€

Les Fables de La Fontaine restaurant   Seafood
131 rue St-Dominique, 7e. tel. 01 44 18 37 55
www.lesfablesdelafontaine.net
Notes: €€€€. Advance reservations preferable. In the Palais neighborhood.

Restaurant Mariette restaurant   French
24 rue Bosquet, 7e.   tel. 01 45 51 78 82   www.restaurant-
mariette.com
Notes: € - €€. "yes of course". No advance reservations necessary.

Vine et Maree-Voltaire restaurant   Seafood
71 avenue de Suffren, 7e.   tel. 01 47 83 27 12
http://www.vin-et-maree.com/
Notes: €€€€. No advance notice necessary. "Just come."

Naturalia La Motte Picquet   health food store
38 avenue de la Motte Picquet, 7e.

Aux Ducs de Bourgogne Crêperie   creperie
30 rue de Bourgogne, 7e.   tel. 01 45 51 32 48
Notes: €. This is recommended by fellow celiacs, but make sure to confirm
that your particular order is gluten-free.

8^E ARRONDISSEMENT

Bocconi   restaurant   Italian
10 bis rue d'Artois, 8e.   tel. 01 53 76 44 44 www.trattoria-bocconi.fr
Notes: €€€€. GF pasta on hand.

Chez Francis   restaurant   French
7 place de l'Alma, 8e.   tel. 01 82 28 77 39
www.chezfrancis-restaurant.com
Notes: €€€

Dominique Bouchet   restaurant   Classic French
11 rue Treilhard, 8e.   tel. 01 45 61 09 46   www.dominique-bouchet.com
Notes: €€€€

La Fermette Marbeuf 1900 restaurant   Brasserie
5 rue Marbeuf, 8e.   tel. 01 53 23 08 00
Notes: €€€

Le Bristol   restaurant   French
112 rue du Faubourg Saint-Honoré, 8e.   tel. 01 53 43 43 42
lebristolparis.com
Notes: €€€€

Le Cinq   restaurant   haute French
31 avenue George V, 8e.   tel. 01 49 52 70 00   www.fourseasons.com
Notes: €€€€. GF bread available too! In the Four Seasons hotel. Average
dinner for one €100.

Le Safran Restaurant   restaurant   French
51/57 rue de Courcelles, 8e.   tel. 01 58 36 67 00 http://www.hilton.co.uk
Notes: €€€€. Located in Hilton Hotel. Will serve GF with advance notice.

Leon de Bruxelles   restaurant   Belgian
63 av des Champs-Elysées, 8e.   tel. 01 42 25 96 16
www.leon-de-bruxelles.fr
Notes: €€€. This restaurant is part of a large chain all over France. They have
limited items that are GF, but their Director of Quality Control nationwide
provided us with a list of menu items that are GF. See page 16.

Maxim's   restaurant   French Classic
3 rue Royale, 8e.   tel. 01 42 65 27 94   www.maxims-de-paris.com
Notes: €€€€

Pierre Gagnaire   restaurant   Modern French
6 rue Balzac, 8e.   tel. 01 58 36 12 50   www.pierre-gagnaire.com
Notes: €€€€. Extremely expensive. In the Hotel Balzac.

Senderens   restaurant   brasserie
9 place de la Madelein, 8e.   tel. 01 42 65 22 90   www.senderens.fr
Notes: €€€€

Spoon Food and Wine   restaurant   International
14 rue Marignan, 8e.   tel. 01 40 76 34 44   www.spoon.tm.fr
Notes: €€€€. Reservations essential.

Taillevent   restaurant   French
15 rue Lemennais 8E, 8e.   tel. 01 44 95 15 01   www.taillevent.com
Notes: €€€€. Reservations essential. Jacket and tie required.entrées €34-€90.

Hilton Arc de Triomphe Paris hotel   hotel with one restaurant   French
51/57 rue de Courcelles, 8e.   tel. 01 58 36 67 00   http://www.hilton.co.uk
Notes: €€€€. Will serve GF room service with Advance notice. Also has a
restaurant.

La Vie Claire   health food store   85 boulevard Haussman, 8e.
Naturalia   health food store   21 bd des Batignolles, 8e.

Cojean Marbeuf   Fast, healthy food   GF soups and salads
19 rue Clement Marot, 8e.   tel. 01 47 20 44 10   www.cojean.fr
Notes: €. Open Monday-Friday 8:30-7

Cojean Mathurins   Fast, healthy food   GF soups and salads
64 rue des Mathurins, 8e.   tel. 01 49 24 09 24   www.cojean.fr
Notes: €. Open Monday-Friday 10-4

Cojean Miromesnil   Fast, healthy food   GF soups and salads
11 avenue Delcassé, 8e.   tel. 01 53 76 39 69   www.cojean.fr
Notes: €. Open Monday-Friday 8-6

Arc de Triomphe (J.Clayton)

Cojean Monceau   Fast, healthy food   GF soups and salads
32 rue Monceau, 8e.   tel. 01 42 89 05 12   www.cojean.fr
Notes: €. Open Monday-Friday 10-3

Cojean Roosevelt   Fast, healthy food   GF soups and salads
55 avenue Franklin Delano Roosevelt, 8e.   tel. 01 45 63 19 09
www.cojean.fr
Notes: €. Open Monday-Saturday 10-4

Cojean Washington   Fast, healthy food   GF soups and salads
25 rue Washington, 8e. tel. 01 45 61 07 33   www.cojean.fr
Notes: €. Open Monday-Friday 10-4

9^E ARRONDISSEMENT

Au Petit Riche   restaurant   Bistro, classic French
25 rue le Peletier, 9e.   tel. 01 47 70 68 68   www.aupetitriche.com
Notes: €€€€

Autour du Saumon   restaurant   Seafood
56 rue des Martyrs, 9e.   tel. 01 48 70 47 58 http://autourdusaumon.eu
Notes: €€. This establishment is take away only. There are three restaurants in Paris as part of this chain.

Café de la Paix   restaurant   French Classic
12 bd des Capucines, 9e.   tel. 01 40 07 36 36   www.cafedelapaix.fr
Notes: €€€€. Will serve GF with advance notice.

Casa Olympe   restaurant   New French
48 rue St-Georges, 9e.   tel. 01 42 85 26 01   www.casaolympe.com
Notes: €€€€. .€28-€35.

Charlot - Roi des Coquillages restaurant   brasserie
12 pl de Clichy, 9e.   tel. 01 53 20 48 00   www.charlot-paris.com
Notes: €€€

Georgette   restaurant   Bistro
29 rue St-Georges, 9e.   tel. 01 42 80 39 13
Notes: €€€€. Average dinner for one€40

Hard Rock Café   restaurant   American
14 boulevard Montmartre, 9e.   tel. 01 53 24 60 00 www.hardrockcafe.com
Notes: N/A. No need to call ahead. Staff is very familiar with GF.

Jean   restaurant   New French
8 rue St-Lazare, 9e.   tel. 01 48 70 62 73   www.restaurantjean.fr
Notes: €€€€

La Table d'Anvers   restaurant   Classic French
2 pl d'Anvers, 9e. tel. 01 48 70 35 21   http://www.latabledanvers.com/
Notes: €€

L'Auberge du Clou   restaurant   Classic French
30 av Trudaine, 9e.   tel. 01 48 78 22 48   www.aubergeduclou.fr
Notes: €€€ - €€€€

Le 16 Haussmann   restaurant   New French
16 bd Haussmann, 9e.   tel. 01 44 83 40 58   www.16haussmann.com
Notes: €€€€. with advance notice, they can make GF dishes but a limited selection and not from the regular menu.

Leon de Bruxelles   restaurant   Belgian
8 pl de Clichy, 9e.   tel. 01 48 74 00 43   www.leon-de-bruxelles.fr
Notes: €€€. This restaurant is part of a large chain all over France. They have limited items that are GF, but their Director of Quality Control nationwide provided us with a list of menu items that are GF. See page 16.

Pousse-Pousse   restaurant   bio/vegetarian
7 rue Notre-Dame-de-Lorette, 9e.   tel. 01 53 16 10 81
www.pousse-pousse.eu
Notes: € - €€

Wally Le Saharien   restaurant   North African
36 rue Rodier, 9e.   tel. 01 42 85 51 90
Notes: €€€€. Main entrées €35-€57.

Biocoop Du Faubourg health food store 73 rue Faubourg Poissonnière, 9e.
Naturalia   health food store   43 bd de Clichy, 9e.
Naturalia Lamartine   health food store   37 rue Lamartine, 9e.

Cojean Figaro   Fast, healthy food   GF soups and salads
Siège Social du Figaro 14 boulevard Haussmann, 9e.   tel. 01 57 08 60 18
www.cojean.fr
Notes: €. Open Monday-Friday 8-6

Cojean Haussmann   Fast, healthy food   GF soups and salads
17 boulevard Haussmann, 9e.   tel. 01 47 70 22 65   www.cojean.fr
Notes: €. Open Monday-Friday 8-7

Cojean le Peletier   Fast, healthy food   GF soups and salads
30 rue le Peletier, 9e. tel. 01 48 00 97 50   www.cojean.fr
Notes: €. Open Monday-Friday 10-3

Cojean Madeleine   Fast, healthy food   GF soups and salads
6 rue de Sèze, 9e. tel. 01 40 06 08 80   www.cojean.fr
Notes: €. Open Monday-Friday 8:30-6

Cojean Printemps   Fast, healthy food   GF soups and salads
64 boulevard Haussmann, 9e. tel. 01 42 82 40 25   www.cojean.fr
Notes: €. Open Monday-Saturday 9:35-8, Thursday evening to 10

Cojean Provence   Fast, healthy food   GF soups and salads
66 rue de Provence, 9e.   tel. 01 45 26 25 85   www.cojean.fr
Notes: €. Open Monday-Friday 10-4

10ᴱ ARRONDISSEMENT

La Chandelle Verte   restaurant   bio
40 rue d'Enghien, 10e.   tel. 01 47 70 25 44
Notes: € - €€

Philou   restaurant   French
12 avenue Richerand, 10e.   tel. 01 42 38 00 13
Notes: €€€. Reservations necessary, and announce GF. Very nice staff.

Voy Alimento   restaurant   bio/vegetarian
23 rue des Vinaigriers, 10e.   tel. 01 42 01 03 44   www.voyalimento.fr
Notes: € - €€. 90% of their dishes are GF.

La Vie Claire   health food store   9 /11 place du Colonel Fabien, 10e.
Naturalia Beaurepaire   health food store   24 rue Beaurepaire, 10e.
Naturalia Magenta   health food store   73 boulevard Magenta, 10e.

11ᴱ ARRONDISSEMENT

Afghanistan   restaurant   Afghan
48 rue Saint-Maur, 11e.   tel. 01 49 23 02 91
Notes: €. No advance notice necessary.

Auberge des Pyrenees Cevennes restaurant   French
106 rue de la Folie Mericourt, 11e.   tel. 01 43 57 33 70
Notes: €€€ - €€€€. Advance notice necessary. In the Popincourt district.

Babylone restaurant Middle Eastern
21 rue Daval, 11e. tel. 01 47 00 55 02
Notes: €€. No gluten in dishes.

Chez Imogene restaurant French
25 rue Jean-Pierre Timbaud, 11e. tel. 01 48 07 14 59
http://www.chezimogene.com/
Notes: €. No need to call ahead.

Chez Paul restaurant French
13 rue de Charonne, 11e. tel. 01 47 00 34 57 www.chezpaul.com
Notes: €€€€. No need for Advance notice.

Le Chalet d'Avron restaurant Swiss, fondue
108 rue de Montreuil, 11e. tel. 01 43 71 18 62
lechaletdavron.ex-flash.com
Notes: €. identify to the chef exactly what you can and can't eat. Advance
notice necessary. In the Popincourt district.

Le Grande Mericourt restaurant French
22 rue de la Folie Mericourt, 11e. tel. 01 43 38 94 04
www.legrandmericourt.fr/
Notes: €€€ - €€€€. Call ahead.

Le Melange des Genres restaurant French
44 boulevard Voltaire, 11e. tel. 01 47 00 41 06
Notes: € - €€

Le Tagine restaurant French
13 rue Crussol, 11e. tel. 01 47 00 28 67 www.letagine.fr
Notes: €€€. Identify to the chef exactly what you can and can't eat. Advance
notice necessary. In the Popincourt district.

L'Ecailler du Bistrot restaurant Seafood
22 rue Paul-Bert, 11e. tel. 01 43 72 76 77
Notes: €€ - €€€

Eiffel Tower in the evening (M. Maestra)

Leon de Bruxelles   restaurant   Belgian
8 pl de la République, 11e.   tel. 01 43 38 28 69 www.leon-de-bruxelles.fr
Notes: €€€. This restaurant is part of a large chain all over France. They have
limited items that are GF, but their Director of Quality Control nationwide
provided us with a list of menu items that are GF. See page 16.

Les Galopins   restaurant   French
33 Philippe Auguste, 11e.   tel. 01 43 67 01 23   www.lesgalopins.fr/
Notes: €€ - €€€. Advance notice necessary.

Loving Hut   restaurant   bio/vegetarian
92 boulevard Beaumarchais, 11e.   tel. 01 48 06 43 84 paris.lovinghut.fr
Notes: €. Advance notice preferable.

Soya   restaurant   bio/vegetarian
20 rue de la Pierre Levée, 11e.   tel. 01 48 06 33 02   www.soya75.fr
Notes: €. GF dishes indicated on menu.

The Greenhouse restaurant Irish
43 rue Godefroy Cavaignac, 11e. tel. 01 43 72 35 75
Notes: €. English spoken.

Vine et Maree-Voltaire restaurant Seafood
276 boulevard Voltaire, 11e. tel. 01 43 72 31 23
http://www.vin-et-maree.com/
Notes: €€€€. No advance notice necessary. "Just come."

Biocoop Le Retour health food store 114 avenue Philippe Auguste, 11e.
Biocoop Lemo health food store 33 boulevard Voltaire, 11e.
Biosphare health food store 57 rue Saint Maur, 11e.
La Vie Claire health food store 42 boulevard du Temple, 11e.
La Vie Claire health food store 255 boulevard Voltaire, 11e.
Naturalia health food store 33 rue de la Roquette, 11e.
Naturalia health food store 119 rue de Montreuil, 11e.
Naturalia Richard Lenoir health food store 108 bd Richard Lenoir, 11e.
Naturalia Voltaire health food store 196 bd Voltaire, 11e.

12^E ARRONDISSEMENT

Cafe Barge restaurant French
5 Port de la Rapee, 12e. tel. 01 40 02 09 09 www.cafebarge.com
Notes: €€ - €€€. With advance notice, they can make GF dishes.

Biocoop Paris 12Ème health food store 47 rue Jacques Hillairet, 12e.
Naturalia Bizot health food store 72-74 ave du Général Michel Bizot, 12e.

13^E ARRONDISSEMENT

Auberge Etchégorry restaurant Southwest French
41 rue Croulebarbe, 13e. tel. 01 44 08 83 51 www.etchegorry.com
Notes: €€€. Advance notice necessary.

Buffalo Grill restaurant American steakhouse
2 rue Raymond Aron, 13e. tel. 01 45 86 76 71 www.buffalo-grill.fr
Notes: € - €€. "Just come."

Chez Paul restaurant Bistro
22 rue de la Butte aux Cailles, 13e. tel. 01 45 89 22 11
Notes: €€€€. No advance notice necessary.

La Bambou Vietnamese Restaurant   restaurant   Vietnamese
70 rue Baudricourt, 13e.   tel. 01 45 70 91 75
Notes: €€

L'Aimant du Sud   restaurant   Classic French
40 bd Arago, 13e.   tel. 01 47 07 33 57
Notes: €€. "No problem! Just come." Very nice staff.

L'Avant Goût   restaurant   New French
26 rue Bobillot, 13e.   tel. 01 53 80 24 00   www.lavantgout.com
Notes: €€€. No advance notice necessary. Average dinner for one €43.

Le Petit Marguery   restaurant   bistro
9 bd de Port-Royal, 13e.   tel. 01 43 31 58 59   www.petitmarguery.com
Notes: €€€€. No advance notice necessary.

Le Temps des Cerises   restaurant   Bistro
18 rue de la Butte aux Cailles, 13e.   tel. 01 45 89 69 48
Notes: €€. "Just come."

Paradis Thai   restaurant   Thai
132 rue de Tolbiac, 13e.   tel. 01 45 83 22 26   www.paradisthai.com
Notes: N/A. A limited number dishes are GF.

Biocoop Paris Glaciere   health food store   55 rue de la Glacière, 13e.
Naturalia   health food store   44 av Italie, 13e.
Naturalia Tolbiac   health food store   71 rue de Tolbiac, 13e.

EXKi Av de France   Fast, healthy food
116 Av de France, 13e.   www.exki.fr
Notes: Some dishes have been labeled "SF" or "sans gluten.".

14^E ARRONDISSEMENT

La Cagouille   restaurant   Seafood
10 pl Constantin Brancusi, 14e.   tel. 01 43 22 09 01 www.la-cagouille.fr
Notes: €€€€. Advance notice necessary.

La Cerisaie   restaurant   Southwest French
70 bd Edgar Quinet, 14e.   tel. 01 43 20 98 90
Notes: €€. "Just come."

La Maison Courtine   restaurant   Southwest French
157 av du Maine, 14e.   tel. 01 45 43 08 04   www.lamaisoncourtine.com
Notes: €€€ - €€€€. "Just come." Average dinner for one €35.

La Régalade   restaurant   basque
49 av Jean Moulin, 14e.   tel. 01 45 45 65 80
Notes: €€€€. "Yes, absolutely!" Reservations necessary.

Le Bistrot du Dôme   restaurant   Seafood
1 rue Delambre, 14e.   tel. 01 43 35 32 00
Notes: €€. "Just come."

Le Duc   restaurant   Seafood
243 bd Raspail, 14e.   tel. 01 43 20 96 30
Notes: €€€€. "Just come." Average dinner for one €81.

Leon de Bruxelles   restaurant   Belgian
82 bis bd du Montparnasse, 14e.   tel. 01 43 21 66 62
www.leon-de-bruxelles.fr
Notes: €€€. This restaurant is part of a large chain all over France. They have limited items that are GF, but their Director of Quality Control nationwide provided us with a list of menu items that are GF. See page 16.

Pasco   restaurant   Mediterranean
74 bd de la Tour Maubourg, 14e.   tel. 01 44 18 33 26
www.restaurantpasco.com
Notes: €€€. Advance reservations preferable. In the Palais neighborhood.

Vine et Maree-Voltaire   restaurant   Seafood
108 ave du Maine, 14e.   tel. 01 43 20 29 50   www.vin-et-maree.com
Notes: €€€€. No advance notice necessary. "Just come."

Bio Paris Catalogne   health food store   2 place de Catalogne, 14e.
L'Elan Nature   health food store   107 Bis rue Gen Leclerc, 14e.
Naturalia Brezin   health food store   13 rue Brézin, 14e.

EXKi Bd Montparnasse   Fast, healthy food
82 Bd Montparnasse, 14e.   www.exki.fr
Notes: €. Some dishes have been labeled "SF" or "sans gluten."

Le Louvre (J.Clayton)

15^E ARRONDISSEMENT

Atelier Aubrac   restaurant   French
51 Bld. Garibaldi, 15e.   tel. 01 45 66 96 78 www.atelieraubrac.com/fr
Notes: €. Very nice staff.

Autour du Saumon   restaurant   seafood
116 rue de la Convention, 15e.   tel. 01 45 54 31 16
http://autourdusaumon.eu
Notes: €€ - €€€. English spoken.

Banyan   restaurant   Thai
24 place Etienne Pernet, 15e.   tel. 01 40 60 09 31
Notes: €€€ - €€€€. "Just come."

Cave de l'Os à Moëlle   restaurant   Classic French
181 rue de Lourmel, 15e.   tel. 01 45 57 28 28
Notes: €€€€. English spoken. Very accommodating. No advance notice
necessary.€28-€35.

Chez Papa   restaurant   Southwest French
101 rue de la Croix Nivert, 15e.   tel. 01 48 28 31 88 www.chezpapa.fr
Notes: € - €€. "Just come."

Erawan   restaurant   Thai
76 rue de la Fédération, 15e.   tel. 01 47 83 55 67
Notes: €€€€

La Gauloise   restaurant   Bistro
59 av de la Motte-Picquet, 15e.   tel. 01 47 34 11 64
Notes: €€€€

La Villa Corse   restaurant   Corsica
164 bd de Grenelle, 15e.   tel. 01 53 86 70 81   www.lavillacorse.com
Notes: €€€ - €€€€

L'Atelier du Parc   restaurant   French
35 Bd Lefebvre, 15e.   tel. 01 42 50 68 85   www.atelierduparc.
Notes: €€

Le Troquet   restaurant   New French, Basque
21 rue François Bonvin, 15e.   tel. 01 45 66 89 00
Notes: €€€€

Restaurant de la Tour   restaurant   Classic French
6 rue Desaix, 15e.   tel. 01 43 06 04 24 www.restaurant-delatour.fr
Notes: €€ - €€€. Call ahead so the chef can have something ready for you.

Biocoop Grenelle	health food store	44 bd de Grenelle, 15e.
La Vie Claire	health food store	20 rue de l'Eglise, 15e.
La Vie Claire	health food store	60 rue Brancion, 15e.
Naturalia	health food store	332 rue Lecourbe, 15e.
Naturalia Cambronne	health food store	86 rue de Cambronne, 15e.
Naturalia Convention	health food store	222 rue de la Convention, 15e.

16^E ARRONDISSEMENT

Bon   restaurant   Asian
25 rue de la Pompe, 16e.   tel. 01 40 72 70 00   www.restaurantbon.fr
Notes: €€€. GF items are highlighted in different color on the regular menu.

Fakhr el Dine   restaurant   Lebanese
30 rue de Longchamp, 16e.   tel. 01 47 27 90 00   www.fakhreldine.com
Notes: €€€€

Giulio Rebellato   restaurant   Italian
136 rue de la Pompe, 16e.   tel. 01 47 27 50 26   www.giulio-rebellato.com
Notes: €€€ - €€€€

La Grande Cascade   restaurant   haute French
Allée de Longchamp, 16e.   tel. 01 45 27 33 51   www.grandecascade.com
Notes: €€€€

La Table Lauriston   restaurant   bistro
129 rue Lauriston, 16e.   tel. 01 47 27 00 07
Notes: €€€€. Average €50.

La Villa Corse   restaurant   Corsica
141 avenue Malakoff, 16e.   tel. 01 40 67 18 44   www.lavillacorse.com
Notes: €€€ - €€€€

L'Astrance   restaurant   French
4 rue Beethoven, 16e.   tel. 01 40 50 84 40
Notes: €€€. entrées €24-€38.

Le Bec Rouge   restaurant   French
46 bd du Montparnasse, 16e.   tel. 01 42 22 45 54
Notes: €€€€. "Of course, no problem. Just come."

Le Petit Pergolèse   restaurant   Bistro, new French
38 rue Pergolèse, 16e.   tel. 01 45 00 23 66
Notes: €€€€

Le Pré Catelan   restaurant   haute French
Bois de Boulogne route de Suresnes, 16e.   tel. 01 44 14 41 14
www.precatelanparis.om
Notes: €€€€

Prunier   restaurant   seafood
16 av Victor Hugo, 16e.   tel. 01 44 17 35 85   www.prunier.com
Notes: €€€€. Advance notice necessary. Very nice and very accommodating
staff.

Vine et Maree-Voltaire   restaurant   Seafood
183 boulevard Murat, 16e.   tel. 01 46 47 91 39   www.vin-et-maree.com
Notes: €€€€. No advance notice necessary. "Just come."

La Vie Claire   health food store   25 rue de l'Annonciation, 16e.
Naturalia Sablons   health food store   25 rue des Sablons, 16e.

Cojean kléber   GF soups and salads   French
78 avenue Kléber, 16e.   tel. 01 47 04 73 80 www.cojean.fr
Notes: €. Open Monday-Friday 8-4.

17^E ARRONDISSEMENT

da zavola   restaurant   Italian
11 rue Brochant, 17e.   tel. 01 58 59 36 91   www.dazavola.com
Notes: N/A. Not many GF dishes but they do have GF gnocchi.

Guy Savoy   restaurant   French
18 rue Troyon, 17e.   tel. 01 43 80 40 61   www.guysavoy.com
Notes: €€€€. Reservations essential.

La Bonne Heure   restaurant   French
11 rue Brochant, 17e.   tel. 01 46 27 49 89   http://la-bonneheure.fr/
Notes: €. Advance notice necessary

Le Bistro du 17eme   restaurant   French
108 avenue de Villiers, 17e.   tel. 01 47 63 32 77   www.bistrocie.fr
Notes: €€€ - €€€€. Reservations necessary.

Le Manoir   restaurant   French
7 rue des Moines, 17e.   tel. 01 46 27 54 51
Notes: €. Call ahead. Many celiac clients.

Leon de Bruxelles   restaurant   Belgian
95 bd Gouvion-St-Cyr, 17e.   tel. 01 55 37 95 30 www.leon-de-bruxelles.fr
Notes: €€€. This restaurant is part of a large chain all over France. They have
limited items that are GF, but their Director of Quality Control nationwide
provided us with a list of menu items that are GF. See page 16.

Saidoune   restaurant   Lebanese
35 rue Legendre, 17e.   tel. 01 47 63 83 08   www.saidoune.com
Notes: € - €€. Advance notice necessary

Un des Sens   restaurant   French
10 rue du Cheroy, 17e.   tel. 01 42 93 10 11 www.undessens.net
Notes: N/A. Many celiac clients and many GF products. No advanced
necessary. Very nice staff.

Biocoop Paris	health food store	153 rue Legendre, 17e.
Naturalia	health food store	107 Bis av de St Ouen, 17e.
Naturalia Bayen	health food store	11 rue Bayen, 17e.
Naturalia Levis	health food store	16 rue Levis, 17e.

18^E ARRONDISSEMENT

Au Grain de Folie   restaurant   bio
24 rue La Vieuville, 18e.   tel. 01 42 58 15 57
Notes: €

Bistro Poulbot   restaurant   French
39 rue Lamarck, 18e.   tel. 01 46 06 86 00
Notes: €€. Advance notice necessary.

Chez Toinette   restaurant   bistro
20 rue Germain Pilon, 18e.   tel. 01 42 54 44 36
Notes: €€. Advance notice necessary.

Des Si & Des Mets Restaurant   restaurant   French gluten-free!
63 rue Lepic, 18e.   tel. 01 42 55 19 61   www.dessietdesmets.com
Notes: €€. GFM (see sample menu at end of section).

Just Brigitte plus Elsa Just B   fusion   bistro
46 rue Caulaincourt, 18e.   tel. 01 42 55 14 25
Notes: €€. English speakers and knowledgeable about GF.

Sacre Coeur (J. Clayton)

La Famille restaurant French
41 rue des Trois Freres, 18e. tel. 01 42 52 11 12
Notes: €€. Very highly recommended. The chef comes from a macrobiotic restaurant and, exit for one dessert left over from the old chef, cooks with absolutely no gluten. Reservations necessary. English spoken.

La Taverne de Montmartre restaurant French
rue Gabrielle no 25, 18e. tel. 01 46 06 88 48
Notes: €€ - €€€. Advance notice necessary.

L'Assiette restaurant Modern French
78 rue Labat, 18e. tel. 01 42 59 06 63
Notes: €€€. Advance notice necessary.entrées €21-€37.

le crep'uscule restaurant French
91 rue Lamarck, 18e. tel. 01 42 64 29 20
Notes: €€€. Very small. Reservations essential.

Le Jardin d'en Face restaurant French
33 rue des Trois Freres, 18e. tel. 01 53 28 00 75
Notes: €€ - €€€. Advance notice necessary.

Lui l'insolent restaurant French
15 rue Caulaincourt, 18e. tel. 01 53 28 28 31
Notes: €€. Advance notice necessary.

Marguerite restaurant French
50 rue de Clignancourt, 18e. tel. 01 42 51 66 18
www.marguerite-resto.com
Notes: €€ - €€€. Reservations necessary.

Naturalia	health food store	37 rue du Poteau, 18e.
Naturalia	health food store	41 rue Lepic, 18e.
Naturalia	health food store	118 rue Caulaincourt, 18e.

19[E] ARRONDISSEMENT

Buffalo Grill restaurant American steakhouse
29 av Corentin Cariou, 19e. tel. 01 40 36 21 41 www.buffalo-grill.fr
Notes: € - €€. This restaurant chain has a list of gluten-free foods along with a list of other allergen free foods.

Café de la Musique   restaurant   Classic French
213 av Jean Jaurès, 19e.   tel. 01 48 03 15 91   www.cite-musique.fr
Notes: N/A. Advance notice necessary.

Chez Vincent   restaurant   Italian
Parc des Buttes Chaumont, 19e.   tel. 01 42 02 22 45
Notes: €€€. Advance notice necessary.

La Cave Gourmande (Restaurant de Mark Singer)   restaurant   Bistro
10 rue du Général Brunet, 19e.   tel. 01 40 40 03 30
Notes: €€€€. "Just come." Average dinner for one €49.

Lao Siam   restaurant   Thai
49 rue de Belleville, 19e.   tel. 01 40 40 09 68
Notes: €€€ - €€€€. "Just come." Very nice staff.

Canal Bio   health food store   46 bis Quai de la Loire, 19e.
Naturalia Meaux   health food store   59 rue de Meaux, 19e.

20ᴱ ARRONDISSEMENT

Baratin   restaurant   French
3 rue Jouye-Rouve, 20e.   tel. 01 43 49 39 70
Notes: €€€ - €€€€. "Just come." Extremely nice staff. They have many
sauces that "never have gluten".

La Boulangerie   restaurant   Bistro
15 rue des Panoyaux, 20e.   tel. 01 43 58 45 45
Notes: €€€ - €€€€. Advance notice necessary. Many celiac clients.

Le Zéphyr   restaurant   Bistro
1 rue du Jourdain, 20e.   tel. 01 46 36 65 81 www.lezephyrcafe.com
Notes: €€. Advance notice necessary.

Les Allobroges   restaurant   Classic French
71 rue des Grands-Champs, 20e.   tel. 01 43 73 40 00
Notes: €€€€. "Of course!"

Coté Parvis   restaurant/brasserie   French
2 place de la Défense CNIT - BP 210   tel. 01 46 92 10 10
http://www.hilton.co.uk
Notes: €€€€

Hilton Paris La Défense hotel   hotel with one restaurant   French
2 place de la Défense CNIT - BP 210   tel. 01 46 92 10 10
http://www.hilton.co.uk
Notes: €€€€

Biocoop Belleville En Bio · health food store   62 rue de Belleville, 20e.
La Vie Claire   health food store   13 bis ave du Père Lachaise, 20e.
La Vie Claire   health food store   305 rue des Pyrenees, 20e.
Naturalia Jourdain   health food store   2 rue du Jourdain, 20e.
Naturalia Pyrenees   health food store   180 bis rue des Pyrénées, 20e.

SAMPLE MENU FROM

DES SI ET DES METS

(menu changes monthly)
ALL ITEMS ARE GLUTEN-FREE AND MOST ARE LACTOSE-FREE

STARTERS (€7)
Cream of chestnuts
Fresh mushrooms, fresh fennel raw
Salad with crunchy vegetables
Bunch of leeks and beetroot, sherry coulis

MAIN DISHES (€ 16-20)
Exotic stew of lamb and artichokes
Ballotine chicken with preserved lemon and sesame, with its own vegetable tian
Salmon with crispy rice cake, accompanied by mashed potatoes and herbs
Penne with saffron vegetables
Jacques scallops with coffee-flavored breadcrumbs, mango sauce and risotto with
zucchini * (+2 € in the menu)

DESSERTS (€7-8)
Chocolate fondue and pears
Hot and cold plums and mangoes in speculos
Cheesecake * (+2 € in the menu)
Panna cotta with lemon, and flowing raspberry hearts
Cheese Platter * (+2 € in the menu)

BRUNCH MENU (€22) (Sunday lunch only)
Coffee or tea or chocolate
Orange juice or smoothies   (Supplement 2 €)
Toast, pears and chocolate fondant cake with banana and honey
Choice of: Hamburger House / Salmon Tartar / Quiche Lorraine / Vegetable Quiche
All our dishes are served with fried potatoes and salad, cottage cheese

CHILDREN'S MENU 12 € (- 10 years)
Supreme of chicken and vegetable tian OR
Salmon fillet, mashed potatoes
Chocolate fondue or cottage cheese coated pears, mango coulis
Beverage choices

THE REST OF THE ÎLE-DE-FRANCE

Keeping watch at Versailles (B. Susa)

DISNEYLAND® PARK PARIS

If you find yourself going to Disneyland Paris, you can rest assured that there are adequate GF meals for you to consume at all of the restaurants in the park. The following information is condensed from the the French celiac Society website and the Disneyland Paris website (specifically see www.disneylandparis.co.uk/UK/EN/Neutral/Images/food_allergies_uk.pdf and http://www.magicalkingdoms.com/dlp/dining/diets.html

---

In **Disneyland** you can contact 2 dieticians:
Ms. FAULIN Adoracion & Ms. FAULIN Johanna
email: dlp.dietetique@disney.com
tel. 33 (0)1 64 74 39 78   fax: 33 (0)1 64 74 38 13
They can order you a gluten-free meal (on a tray) that you will eat in certain restaurants of the place.

The Resort's special allergen-free meals by Natama cover nearly 60 food allergies, are guaranteed by the supplier, and are served in all of the restaurants (table service and buffet-style) in Disney Hotels and the Park. The restaurants offer one starter, a choice of four main courses and a choice of three desserts. The list of ingredients used is exhaustive (meaning that there are no "hidden" ingredients).

Choose your meal in the selection, available at the restaurants listed on the following page. No pre-reservation is necessary. If you would like to have lunch or dinner at one of the table service or buffet-style restaurants, advance reservations are recommended.

Contact Central Restaurant Reservation Service at +33 (0) 1 60 30 40 50 and tell the agent which foods you are allergic to. When you arrive at the restaurant, speak to one of the managers, who will inform you of the selection of meals currently available.

Disneyland® Paris shall not be held liable in the event that you or a child under your care were to consume a meal and/or food or beverage items other than those listed herein if said consumption were to result in an allergic reaction. Note: If your booking concerns a hotel not included in the Disney park, you should contact the hotel directly.

SAMPLE "ALLERGEN-FREE" MEAL
AVAILABLE AT DISNEYLAND® PARK PARIS:

STARTER

Cream of tomato soup: Tomatoes, potatoes, virgin olive oil, sugar, basil, salt, pepper.

MAIN COURSE choose from

Chicken drumsticks, rice: Precooked rice, chicken drumsticks, olive oil, salt, thyme.

Minced beef, carrot purée: Carrot, beef, potato, water, olive oil, salt, pepper, thyme.

Oriental meatballs: Precooked corn meal, meatballs (beef, salt), tomato, courgette, carrot, olive oil, salt

Lamb and vegetables: Courgette, lamb steak (lamb, water, mint, salt), apple, rice flour, carrot, olive oil, salt, pepper

DESSERT choose from

Peach delight: Apple, peach purée (peach,sugar), sugar.

Pom' pom: Apple, sugar.

Caramelised pears: Pears, sugar.

ALLERGENIC FOODS **NOT** USED IN ANY DISNEYLAND® PARK MEALS:

Additives

all types Spelt

Almonds

Apples, uncooked

Avocado

Bananas

Barley

beans

Brazil nuts

Broad beans

Buckwheat

Cashew nuts

Celery

Cherries

Chestnuts

Chick peas

Chilli pepper

Cinnamon

Coconut

Eggs

Fennel

Fish

Gluten

Hazelnuts

Kidney

Kiwi

Lentils

Linseed

Lupin

Macadamia nuts

Melon

Milk

Mushrooms

Mustard

Oats

Peaches, uncooked

Peanut

Peas

Pecans

Pine nuts

Pineapple

Pistachio

Pork

Rabbit

Raspberry, uncook

Rye

Sesame

Shellfish

Soy

Sulphites

Sunflower

Vanilla

Walnuts

Wheat

LIST OF RESTAURANTS OFFERING GLUTEN-FREE MEALS IN DISNEYLAND® PARK:

Walt Disney Studios® Park
Rendez-vous des stars®
Restaurant En Coulisse
Backlot Express restaurant

Disney Village
La Grange at Billy Bob's country western saloon is a service buffet
La légende de Buffalo Bill is a dinner show

Disneyland® Park:

Table Service:
ADVENTURELAND: Blue Lagoon Restaurant
FRONTIERLAND: Silver Spur Steakhouse
MAIN STREET, USA: Walt's – an American Restaurant

Buffet restaurants:
FRONTIERLAND: The Lucky Nugget Saloon
FANTASYLAND: Auberge de Cendrillon
MAIN STREET, USA: Plaza Gardens Restaurant

Counter/Self Service:
ADVENTURELAND: Colonel Hathi's Pizza Outpost
Restaurant Hakuna Matata
FRONTIERLAND: Fuente del Oro Restaurante
Last Chance Café
MAIN STREET, USA: Casey's Corner
FANTASYLAND: Au Chalet de la Marionnette
DISCOVERYLAND: Café Hyperion

Disney hotels at Disneyland Resort Paris
All of the restaurants (Table Service, Buffet-style and Counter/Self Service) at our "Disney's" hotels offer special meals by Natama for food allergy sufferers.

**LIST OF DISNEYLAND® PARK HOTELS
OFFERING GLUTEN-FREE BREAKFASTS:**

Disneyland® Hotel
Disney's New York Hotel®
Disney's Newport Bay Club ®
Disney's Sequoia Lodge ®
Disney's Cheyenne Hotel ®
Disney's Santa Fe Hotel ®
Disney's Davy Crockett Ranch ® (let the front desk staff know about
your special dietary needs when you arrive)
Plaza Gardens Restaurant (breakfast with the Disney characters)
Au Chalet de la Marionnette (Good Morning Fantasyland)

RESERVATIONS AND ACCOMODATIONS
FOR YOUR ENTIRE STAY/VISIT IN THE
PARK CAN BE ARRANGED BY CALLING

(0)1 60 30 40 50 or going to the website:

www.disneylandparis.com

Île-de-France
ANTONY

Biocoop Antony	health food store	88 ave Aristide Briand
La Vie Claire	health food store	38 ave de la Division Leclerc

ARCUEIL

Marriott Courtyard Paris Arcueil   hotel with 1 restaurant
6 avenue President Salvadore Allende ·   tel. 01 77 01 21 21
www.marriott.com/hotels/hotel-information/restaurant/parac-courtyard-paris-arcueil/
Notes: €€€€. will serve GF with advance notice.

Oleo Pazzo Mediterranean Bistro   bistro in Marriott hotel   bistro
6 avenue President Salvadore Allende ·   tel. 01 77 01 21 21
www.marriott.com/hotels/hotel-information/restaurant/parac-courtyard-paris-arcueil/
Notes: €€€€. will serve GF with advance notice.

ARGENTEUIL

La Vie Claire   health food store 19 rue Paul Vaillant Couturier

AULNAY SOUS BOIS

La Vie Claire   health food store   15 avenue Dumont

AUVERS-SUR-OISE

Hostellerie du Nord Restaurant   hotel/restaurant   French
6 rue du General de Gaulle   tel. 01 30 36 70 74 www.hostelleriedunord.fr
Notes: €€ - €€€

AVON

Biocoop Avon Fontainebleau   health food store 1-3 ave Général de Gaulle

BAILLY-ROMAINVILLIERS

Marriott's Village d'Ile-de-France   hotel with 2 restaurants   French
Allee de l'Orme Rond ·   tel. 01 60 42 90 00
www.marriott.com/hotels/travel/pardp-marriotts-village-dlle-de-france
Notes: €€€€. With advance notice, GF breakfast. In Disneyland area.

BARBIZON

Hotel restaurant La Clé d'Or Barbizon   hotel/restaurant   French
73 Grande Rue   tel. 01 60 66 40 96
Notes: €€€€. No breakfast. No advance GF notice necessary.

BOIS COLOMBES

Biocoop Les Bruyeres   health food store   5 rue Hispano Suiza
Naturalia Bois-Colombes health food store   85-89 rue des Bourguignons

BOULOGNE-BILLANCOURT

Naturalia Boulogne   health food store   126 avenue Victor Hugo

BRETIGNY SUR ORGE

La Clayette Bio   health food store
12 rue du Poitou ZAC Maison Neuve

BREUILLET

La Vie Claire   health food store   ZAC rue Buisson Rondau

BRIE COMTE ROBERT

La Vie Claire   health food store   9 rue Gustave Eiffel

BUCHELAY

Leon de Bruxelles   restaurant   Belgian
ZAC du Parc d'Activités des Meuniers   tel. 01 30 94 48 25
www.leon-de-bruxelles.fr
Notes: €€€. This restaurant is part of a large chain all over France. They have limited items that are GF, but their Director of Quality Control nationwide provided us with a list of menu items that are GF. See page 16.

CHAMBOURCY

Bio Chambourcy   health food store
Centre Commercial Le Mail - 50 route de Mantes

CHANTILLY

La Ferme de Conde   restaurant   French
42 Mar Joffre   tel. 03 44 57 32 31
Notes: €€€. Advance notice necessary.

Le Vertugadin   restaurant   French
44 rue Connetable   tel. 03 44 57 03 19
Notes: €€€ - €€€€. English spoken. Reservations needed but no advance GF notice necessary. There are always a few meals on the menu that have no gluten.

CHARENTON

La Vie Claire   health food store   145 bis rue de Paris

Versailles (L. Schulz)

CHARTRES

Le Grand Monarque   restaurant   French
22 place des Epars   tel. 02 37 18 15 15
Notes: €€ - €€€

Le Madrigal   restaurant   brasserie
22 place des Epars   tel. 02 37 18 15 07
Notes: N/A

Le Tripot   restaurant   French
11 place Jean Moulin   tel. 02 37 36 60 11   www.letripot.fr/
Notes: €€ - €€€

Restaurant Le Georges brasserie   Continental
22 rue des Epars   tel. 02 37 18 15 15
Notes: . Advance notice necessary.

CHATILLON
La Vie Claire   health food store   9 avenue Saint Exupery

CHAUMONTEL
La Vie Claire   health food store   RN16 - Immeuble Basika

CHELLES

Le Relais Brunehaut   hotel/restaurant   French
3 rue de l'Eglise   tel. 03 44 42 72 72   www.lerelaisbrunehaut.fr
Notes: €€€ - €€€€

Biocoop Ht Bio   health food store   61 avenue de la Résistance

CHEVRY COSSIGNY

Vergers De Cossigny   health food store   9 allée des Peupliers

CHILLY MAZARIN

Leon de Bruxelles   restaurant   Belgian
ZI de la Butte aux Bergers rue Guynemer   tel. 01 69 01 63 12
www.leon-de-bruxelles.fr
Notes: €€€. This restaurant is part of a large chain all over France. They have limited items that are GF, but their Director of Quality Control nationwide provided us with a list of menu items that are GF. See page 16.

CLICHY LA GARENNE

Naturalia Clichy   health food store   74-76 rue Martre

COLOMBES

Courtyard Paris Defense West - Colombes   hotel with 1 bistro/bar
91 Blvd Charles De Gaulle ·   tel. 01 47 69 59 49
www.marriott.com/hotels/travel/parcf-courtyard-paris-defense-west-colombes/
Notes: €€€€

Oleo Pazzo Bar & Bistro   bistro/bar
91 Blvd Charles De Gaulle ·   tel. 01 47 69 59 49
http://www.marriott.com/hotels/travel/parcf-courtyard-paris-defense-west-colombes/
Notes: €€€. will serve GF with advance notice.

Naturalia Colombes   health food store   7 place Maurice Chavany

COMPIÈGNE

Chez Micheline Restaurant restaurant   French
1 rue Roche | Berny Rivière   tel. 03 23 55 51 25
Notes: . There are many things on the menu that are gluten-free.

CORMEILLES

La Vie Claire   health food store   112 Bd de Pontoise

COULOMMIERS
La Vie Claire   health food store   7 rue de l'Aubetin

COURBEVOIE
Naturalia Courbevoie   health food store   71 rue Armand Silvestre

DAMMARIE LES LYS
La Vie Claire   health food store   753 avenue Marguerite Perey

DEUIL LA BARRE
Eco Bio   health food store   140 bd de Montmorency

ENGHIEN-LES-BAINS
Naturalia Enghien   health food store   58 rue du Général de Gaulle

ERAGNY
Leon de Bruxelles   restaurant   Belgian
N184 1 rue Erables   tel. 01 49 40 02 30   www.leon-de-bruxelles.fr
Notes: €€€. This restaurant is part of a large chain all over France. They have
limited items that are GF, but their Director of Quality Control nationwide
provided us with a list of menu items that are GF. See page 16.

FONTAINEBLEAU
Cote Sud   restaurant   French
1 rue Montebello   tel. 01 64 22 00 33
Notes: €€€€. "We're used to it. Just come."

Croquembouche   restaurant
French
43 rue de France   tel. 01 64 22 01 57
Notes: €€€€

Hamlet   restaurant   French
11 rue Grande   tel. 01 64 22 00 23   www.hamlet-cafe.fr
Notes: €€. Very nice staff. Advance notice necessary.

La Vie Claire   health food store   15 rue des Sablons

GIF SUR YVETTE
La Menthe Poivree   health food store   20 rue Alphonse Pécard

GIVERNY

L'Esquisse Gourmande restaurant   French
73 bis rue Claude Monet   tel. 02 32 51 86 95   www.lesquissegourmande.fr
Notes: €€. "No problem."

GOMETZ LE CHATEL

La Menthe Poivree 2   health food store
Z ne Artisanale des Hautes Vignes Rond Point Saint Nicolas

ISLE ADAM

Leon de Bruxelles   restaurant   Belgian
ZAC du Pont des Rayons Zone du Grand Val   tel. 01 64 97 34 24
www.leon-de-bruxelles.fr
Notes: €€€. This restaurant is part of a large chain all over France. They have
limited items that are GF, but their Director of Quality Control nationwide
provided us with a list of menu items that are GF.

ISSY LES MOULINEAUX

Biocoop Issy   health food store
Queues de cerises 100 ter boulevard Gallieni

ISSY-LES-MOULINEAUX

Naturalia Issy Les Moulinaux health food store   19-21 bd Voltaire

JUVISY ON BARLEY

La Vie Claire   health food store   1 rue Draveil

LE CHESNAY

Biocoop Le Chesnay   health food store   place du 18 juin 9 ave Dutartre

LE PERREUX

La Vie Claire   health food store 74 avenue Georges Clémenceau

LE PERREUX

Biocoop Le Perreux   health food store   131 avenue Pierre Brossolette

LE PLESSIS ROBINSON

Biocoop L'Arbre De Vie health food store   5 avenue de la Libération

MONTIGNY LE BRETONNEUX

Pleinchamp Dans La Ville health food store   24 bis place Etienne Marcel

LE RAINCY

Biocoop Le Raincy   health food store   7 rond point Thiers

LES ULIS

La Menthe Poivree 3 health food store rue de l'Aubrac/ave des Cévennes

LISSES

Leon de Bruxelles   restaurant   Belgian
ZAC Le Clos aux Pois - rue de la Closerie   tel. 01 30 76 00 17
www.leon-de-bruxelles.fr
Notes: €€€. This restaurant is part of a large chain all over France. They have limited items that are GF, but their Director of Quality Control nationwide provided us with a list of menu items that are GF. See page 16.

MAISONS-LAFFITTE

La Vie Claire   health food store   34 rue de Paris

MANTES LA VILLE

Biocoop Du Mantois   health food store   81 avenue Jean Jaurès

MAUREPAS

La Vie Claire   health food store   Leisure Village-3 ave Louis Pasteur

MEAUX

La Vie Claire   health food store   19 rue Ampère

Versailles II (L. Schulz)

MONTGERON

Le Chene   health food store   38 avenue Jean Jaurès

MONTLHERY

Leon de Bruxelles   restaurant   Belgian
RN20 - 113 route d'Orléans   tel. 01 30 50 31 00   www.leon-de-bruxelles.fr
Notes: €€€. This restaurant is part of a large chain all over France. They have limited items that are GF, but their Director of Quality Control nationwide provided us with a list of menu items that are GF. See page 16.

NEUILLY SUR SEINE

Bel Canto   restaurant   French
6 rue du Commandant Pilot   tel. 01 47 47 19 94   www.lebelcanto.com
Notes: €€€€

Leon de Bruxelles   restaurant   Belgian
5 rue de Chartres - Métro Porte Maillot   tel. 01 64 48 93 92
www.leon-de-bruxelles.fr
Notes: €€€. This restaurant is part of a large chain all over France. They have limited items that are GF, but their Director of Quality Control nationwide provided us with a list of menu items that are GF. See page 16.

La Vie Claire   health food store   150 avenue du Roule

NOGENT SUR MARNE

Naturalia Nogent   health food store   68 Grande rue Charles de Gaulle

ORLY AEROGARE CEDEX PARIS

Le Café du Marché   restaurant   French
Orly Sud 267   tel. 01 45 12 45 12   http://www.hilton.co.uk
Notes: €€€€. Located in Hilton Hotel. Will serve GF with advance notice.

Hilton Paris Orly Airport hotel   hotel with one restaurant   French
Orly Sud 267   tel. 01 45 12 45 12   http://www.hilton.co.uk
Notes: €€€€. Will serve GF room service with advance notice.

PARIS LA DEFENSE

Naturalia Cnit   health food store
2 place la Défense CNIT Niveau Jardin

PECQ

La Vie Claire   health food store   8 bis ave du General de Gaulle

PIERREFITTE

Leon de Bruxelles   restaurant   Belgian
106-124 bd Jean Mermoz   tel. 01 30 50 31 00   www.leon-de-bruxelles.fr
Notes: €€€. This restaurant is part of a large chain all over France. They have limited items that are GF, but their Director of Quality Control nationwide provided us with a list of menu items that are GF. See page 16.

PLAISIR

La Vie Claire   health food store   1 avenue Paul Langevin

POISSY

La Vie Claire   health food store   20 avenue du Cep

PONT DE BEZONS

Leon de Bruxelles   restaurant   Belgian
3 esplanade Charles de Gaules   tel. 01 48 54 12 89
www.leon-de-bruxelles.fr
Notes: €€€. This restaurant is part of a large chain all over France. They have limited items that are GF, but their Director of Quality Control nationwide provided us with a list of menu items that are GF. See page 16.

PONTAULT COMBAULT

La Vie Claire   health food store   1 rue du Fort

RAMBOUILLET

Auberge du Louvetier   restaurant   French
19 rue de l' Etang de la Tour   tel. 01 34 85 61 00
www.aubergedulouvetier.com
Notes: €€ - €€€

Bisson Andre   restaurant   Bistro, steakhouse
1 rue General de Gaulle | Yvelines   tel. 01 34 83 04 21
Notes: . There are many things on the menu that are already GF.

La Poste   restaurant   Traditional French
101 rue du General de Gaulle   tel. 01 34 83 03 01
Notes: €€ - €€€. "No problem. We're used to it. Just come."

ROSNY SOUS BOIS

Leon de Bruxelles   restaurant   Belgian
A86 - sortie Rosny centre 32 rue Jules Ferry   tel. 01 30 70 85 50
www.leon-de-bruxelles.fr
Notes: €€€. This restaurant is part of a large chain all over France. They have
limited items that are GF, but their Director of Quality Control nationwide
provided us with a list of menu items that are GF.

RUEIL MALMAISON

Naturalia Rueil Malmaison   health food store   17 rue de Maurepas

RUEIL MALMAISON

Biocoop Rueil Malmaison Rn 13   health food store
286 av. Napoleon Bonaparte

SAINT GERMAIN EN LAYE

L'Epi Dupin   restaurant   French
11 rue Dupin   tel. 01 42 22 64 56   www.epidupin.com
Notes: N/A. "Of course, no problem. "Just come."" In the Luxembourg
neighborhood.

Retour Aux Sources   health food store   2 rue des Sources

SAINT GERMAIN-EN-LAYE

Naturalia Saint Germain En Laye   health food store   33 rue de Poissy

SAINT GIRONS

Bio S'Faire   health food store   15 avenue d'Aulot

SAINT HILAIRE LA VARENNE

La Vie Claire   health food store   2 avenue du Mesnil

SAINT MAUR DES FOSSES

Biocoop Saint-Maur   health food store 26 ter rue du Pont de Créteil

SAINT OUEN

Cojean st ouen   GF soups and salads   French
150 boulevard Victor Hugo   tel. 04 40 10 22 91   www.cojean.fr
Notes: €. Open Monday-Friday 10-3

SAINT OUEN L'AUMONE

Eco Bio Soa   health food store   68 chaussée Jules César

SAINT THIBAULT DES VIGNES

Biocoop Saint Thibault Des Vignes   health food store
Z.A. La Courtillière rue des Marmousets

SARTROUVILLE

Greendy   health food store   57 avenue Maurice Berteaux

SENLIS

L'Hostellerie de la Porte-Bellon   hotel/restaurant   French
51 rue Bellon   tel. 03 44 53 03 05
Notes: €. Advance notice necessary.

SÈVRES

La Vie Claire   health food store   40-44 High Street

SOISY SUR SEINE

La Clairiere   health food store
C. Cial Les Meillottes - rue de l'Ermitage

TRAPPES

Leon de Bruxelles   restaurant   Belgian
55 route de Chartres Zone Immo Parc   tel. 03 44 24 75 39
www.leon-de-bruxelles.fr
Notes: €€€. This restaurant is part of a large chain all over France. They have limited items that are GF, but their Director of Quality Control nationwide provided us with a list of menu items that are GF. See page 16.

TREMBLAY EN FRANCE ROISSY

Les Aviateurs   restaurant   French
Roissypôle rue de Rome   tel. 01 49 19 77 95
Notes: €€€€. In the Hilton Hotel.Will serve GF with advance notice.

Hilton Paris Charles de Gaulle Airport hotel   hotel with 1 restaurant
Roissypôle rue de Rome   tel. 01 49 19 77 77   www.hilton.co.uk
Notes: €€€€. Will serve GF room service with Advance notice. Also has a restaurant.

VAL D'EUROPE SERRIS

La Vie Claire   health food store   4 place de Toscane

VELIZY

Leon de Bruxelles   restaurant   Belgian
Face au Centre Commercial Vélizy 2 ave de l'Europe   tel. 03 26 61 60 00
www.leon-de-bruxelles.fr
Notes: €€€. This restaurant is part of a large chain all over France. They have
limited items that are GF, but their Director of Quality Control nationwide
provided us with a list of menu items that are GF. See page 16.

VERSAILLES

La Perle de Saint-Louis restaurant   French
5 Bis rue Marche Neuf   tel. 01 39 51 50 30
Notes: €€€€

Le Boeuf a la mode   restaurant   French
rue au Pain 4   tel. 01 39 50 31 99 www.leboeufalamode-versailles.com
Notes: € - €€. Many celiac clients.

Le Saint Julien   restaurant   French
6 rue Saint Julien   tel. 01 39 50 00 97   http://www.lesaintjulien.fr/
Notes: N/A. "Just come." Very nice staff.

La Vie Claire   health food store   27 rue des States General
Naturalia Versailles   health food store   88-90 rue de la Paroisse

VINCENNES

Naturalia Vincennes   health food store   188 rue de Fontenay

THE LOIRE VALLEY
(Pays-de-la-Loire)
AND CENTER (CENTRE)

Chenonceaux Castle (M.Rossi)

AMBOISE

La Cene   restaurant   French
52 rue Rabelais   tel. 02 47 57 66 58
Notes: €€

Le Pavillon de Lys   restaurant   French
9 rue d'Orange   tel. 02 47 30 01 01   www.pavillondeslys.com
Notes: €€€€

Le Lion d'Or   hotel, restaurant   French
17 Quai Charles Guinot Amboise   tel. 02 31 92 06 90
www.liondor-bayeux.fr
Notes: €€€

ANGERS

L'Empire   restaurant   French
5 rue St Etienne   tel. 02 41 87 32 00
Notes: €€. Very helpful and English spoken.

Provence Caffe   restaurant   French
9 place du Ralliement   tel. 02 41 87 44 15   www.provence-caffe.com/
Notes: €€. Very helpful.

Une Ile   restaurant   French
9 rue Max Richard   tel. 02 41 19 14 48   www.une-ile.fr/
Notes: €€€€

Biocoop Caba Angers   health food store   122 rue de la Chalouère

AVRILLE

Biocoop Caba Avrille   health food store
30 ter avenue Pierre Mendès France

AZAY-LE-RIDEAU

La Credence   restaurant   French
15 - 17 rue Balzac   tel. 06 28 42 42 20
Notes: N/A

Le Grand Monarque   hotel/restaurant   French
3 place de la Republique   tel. 02 47 45 40 08 www.legrandmonarque.com
Notes: € - €€. Advance notice necessary.

AZE

Biocoop Mayenne Bio Soleil Aze   health food store   2 rue des Aillères

BAGNEUX

La Vie Claire   health food store   Moulin de Bournan

BARJOUVILLE

Leon de Bruxelles   restaurant   Belgian
rue des Pierres Missigault Lieu dit "La Torche"   tel. 02 37 28 69 40
www.leon-de-bruxelles.fr
Notes: €€€. This restaurant is part of a large chain all over France. They have
limited items that are GF, but their Director of Quality Control nationwide
provided us with a list of menu items that are GF. See page 16.

BEAUCOUZE

Leon de Bruxelles   restaurant   Belgian
ZA du Landreau   tel. 02 48 59 23 31   www.leon-de-bruxelles.fr
Notes: €€€. This restaurant is part of a large chain all over France. They have
limited items that are GF, but their Director of Quality Control nationwide
provided us with a list of menu items that are GF. See page 16.

BEAUPREAU

Biocoop Mauges   health food store   4 rue Nicolas Appert

BLOIS

La Vieille Tour   restaurant   French
7 rue Nationale   tel. 02 54 74 67 15   www.vieilletour.fr
Notes: €€ - €€€

Le Castelet   restaurant   French
40 rue Saint-Lubin   tel. 02 54 74 66 09   http://www.le-castelet.eu/
Notes: €€

Le Duc de Guise   restaurant   Italian
13 place Louis XII   tel. 02 54 78 22 39
Notes: €€

L'Epi Vert   health food store   27 rue des Flandres

BOURGES

Leon de Bruxelles   restaurant   Belgian
ZAC de l'échangeur - A71 4 rue Aristide Auxenfans   tel. 03 44 03 00 21
www.leon-de-bruxelles.fr
Notes: €€€. This restaurant is part of a large chain all over France. They have limited items that are GF, but their Director of Quality Control nationwide provided us with a list of menu items that are GF. See page 16.

Bourgeon Vert   health food store   69 rue Barbès

CHALLANS
Biocoop Maraichine   health food store   1 rue de la Cailletière

CHALONNES-SUR-LOIRE
Biocoop Symbiose   health food store   23 place de l'Hôtel de Ville

CHAMBRAY LES TOURS
Leon de Bruxelles   restaurant   Belgian
7 rue Thomas Edison   tel. 01 55 61 24 00   www.leon-de-bruxelles.fr
Notes: €€€. This restaurant is part of a large chain all over France. They have limited items that are GF, but their Director of Quality Control nationwide provided us with a list of menu items that are GF. See page 16.

CHÂTEAU DE USSÉ
Le Clos d'Usse   Inn, restaurant   French
7 rue Principale Rigny-Ussé   tel. 02 47 95 55 47
Notes: €. Will serve dinner and breakfast gluten-free if given advance notice.

CHÂTEAU DE VILLANDRY
Auberge Le Colombien   Inn, restaurant   French
2 rue de la Mairie   tel. 02 47 50 07 27   www.hotel-villandry.com
Notes: €. Will serve dinner and breakfast could free with Advance notice.

CHATEAU D'OLONNE
Biocoop Des Olonnes   health food store   30 rue des Plesses

CHATEAUBRIANT
Biosphere   health food store   67 A rue d'Ancenis

CHENONCEAUX
Le Bon Laboureur   restaurant   French
6 rue Bretonneau   tel. 02 47 23 90 02   www.bonlaboureur.com
Notes: €€ - €€€. Advance notice necessary.

La Roseraie   hotel/restaurant   French
7 rue du Docteur Bretonneau   tel. 02 47 23 90 09
Notes: € - €€

CHEVERNY

St. Hubert   hotel, restaurant   French
122 rue Nationale | Cour-Cheverny   tel. 02 54 79 96 60
www.hotel-sthubert.com
Notes: €€€

CHINON

La Bonne France   restaurant   French
4 place de la Victoire   tel. 02 47 98 01 34   www.labonnefrance.com
Notes: €€

L'Ardoise   restaurant   French
42 rue Rabelais   tel. 02 47 58 48 78
www.lardoise-chinon.com/index.php?option
Notes: N/A. Must phone one day in advance for gluten-free food. Many
celiac customers.

Les Annees 30   restaurant   French, European
78 rue Voltaire   tel. 02 17 93 37 18
Notes: €€€

L'Oceanic   restaurant   Seafood
13 rue Rabelais   tel. 02 47 93 44 55
Notes: €€

CHOLET

Biocoop Soleil Nord   health food store
ZAC de l'Ecuyère 2 rue de la Baie d'Hudson

Biocoop Soleil Sud   health food store   6 av. du Cdt de Champagny

EOURRES

Biocoop Grain De Soleil health food store   Le Village

FONTENAY LE COMTE

Au Pays Bio   health food store
24 rue Louis Auber ZA St Médard des Prés

FONTEVRAUD-L'ABBAYE
Brasserie 'La Fontaine d'Evraud' restaurant   French
place des Plantagenets   tel. 02 41 51 71 11
http://www.hotel-croixblanche.com/menu,brasserie,vin.html
Notes: € - €€

GIEN
Les 7 Saveurs   health food store   197 rue des Fourches

GUERANDE
Les Hameaux Bio   health food store   2 rue des Guérêts

LA BAULE
Castel Marie-Louise   hotel/restaurant   French
1 avenue Andrieu B.P. 409   tel. 02 40 11 48 38
www.relaischateaux.com/marielouise
Notes: €€€€

LA FLECHE
Alterre Native   health food store   12 ave d'Obernkirchen

LA FRESNAYE SUR CHÉDOUET
Auberge Saint Paul   restaurant   cuisine gastronomique
La grande Terre   tel. 02 43 97 82 76   www.auberge-saint-paul.com

LA ROCHE SUR YON
Croq'Bio   health food store   74 rue Montréal – Zone Acti-sud

LAVAL
Biocoop Mayenne Bio Soleil Laval health food store   8 rue Bir Hakeim

LE MANS
Le Fenouil Sud   health food store   21 rue du Circuit

LUISANT
Biocoop Chartres   health food store   43 ave de la République

MANOSQUE
Le Ble En Herbe Zi   health food store   Saint Joseph

MAYENNE
Biocoop Mayenne Bio Soleil health food store   49 bd Lucien de Montigny

MONTARGIS

La Vie Claire   health food store   2 avenue Chautemps

MONTLIVAULT

La Maison d'a Cote   hotel/restaurant   French
25 route de Chambord   tel. 02 54 20 62 30 www.lamaisondacote.fr
Notes: €€€€. GF breakfast too. Advance notice.

MONTLOUIS-SUR-LOIRE

Restaurant La Cave   restaurant   French
69 Quai Albert Baillet   tel. 02 47 45 05 05 www.restaurant-la-cave.com
Notes: €€€ - €€€€

MONTRICHARD

Biocoop Planete Verte health food store   6 rue Victor Hugo

MURS ERIGNE

Biocoop Caba Murs-Erigne health food store   34 route de Cholet

NANTES

La Cigale   restaurant   French
4 place Graslin   tel. 02 51 84 94 94   www.lacigale.com
Notes: €. Ask for a GF meal when you make reservations.in the Graslin-commerce district.

Le Paludier   restaurant   French
2 rue Santeuil   tel. 02 40 69 44 06
Notes: €€ - €€€. Ask for a GF meal when you make reservations.in the Graslin-commerce district.

Leon de Bruxelles   restaurant   Belgian
13 route de Paris   tel. 05 56 49 65 69   www.leon-de-bruxelles.fr
Notes: €€€. This restaurant is part of a large chain all over France. They have limited items that are GF, but their Director of Quality Control nationwide provided us with a list of menu items that are GF. See page 16.

Les Agapes   restaurant   French
17 rue Voltaire   tel. 02 40 89 57 25   www.lesagapes-nantes.fr
Notes: €€€€. "Just come."

Resto Revues   restaurant   French
2 rue du Refuge   tel. 02 40 47 42 91
Notes: N/A. In the Decre-Cathedrale district.

Biocoop Nantes health food store 188 route de Rennes
La Vie Claire health food store rue Pitre Chevalier

OLIVET
Leon de Bruxelles restaurant Belgian
Parc d'Activites des Provinces -45 rue du Berry tel. 02 47 74 66 38
www.leon-de-bruxelles.fr
Notes: €€€. This restaurant is part of a large chain all over France. They have
limited items that are GF, but their Director of Quality Control nationwide
provided us with a list of menu items that are GF.

La Vie Claire health food store 105 rue d'Artois

ORLÉANS
Le Chalut restaurant Seafood
59 rue N-D de Recouvrance tel. 02 38 54 36 36
www.lechalut-orleans.com/
Notes: €€

Le Cosy restaurant French
9 B avenue Paris tel. 02 38 62 89 29
Notes: N/A

Le Girouet restaurant French
14 quai du Châtelet tel. 02 38 81 07 14 www.legirouet.com
Notes: Many GF dishes.

Mosaique restaurant Moroccan
109 rue Faubourg St Jean tel. 02 38 72 11 10 www.restaurantmosaique.fr
Notes: €€€

La Vie Claire health food store Centre commercial - Les halles chatelet

PORNIC
Biocoop Les Hameaux Bio 3 health food store
boulevard du Traité de Paris C.Cial EurysZone de l'Europe

PORNICHET
Biocoop Esprit Bio health food store 4 allée du Courtil Riel

ROMORANTIN LANTHERNAY
La Vie Claire health food store 96 rue Georges Clémenceau

SACHÉ

L'auberge du XIIe siecle   restaurant   French
1 rue du Château   tel. 02 47 26 88 77   accueil.sache.free.fr/auberge.htm
Notes: €€€€

SAINT-DIDIER-SOUSAUBENAS

Les Gatobio   health food store 960 route de Montélimar

SAINT GEREON

Saveur Nature   health food store   104 rue du Bocage

SAINT NAZAIRE

Biocoop Les Hameaux Bio 4   health food store   89 rue Jean Jaurès

SAINT SATURNIN

Leon de Bruxelles   restaurant   Belgian
ZAC des portes de l'Océane rue de Villeneuve   tel. 03 87 51 59 13
www.leon-de-bruxelles.fr
Notes: €€€. This restaurant is part of a large chain all over France. They have limited items that are GF, but their Director of Quality Control nationwide provided us with a list of menu items that are GF. See page 16.

SAINT-SÉBASTIEN-SUR-LOIRE

Biocoop Nantes Sud   health food store   rue Louis Blanc

SANCERRE

La Cote des Monts Damnes restaurant   French
Chavignol   tel. 02 48 54 01 72   www.montsdamnes.com/
Notes: €€€€

Les Augustins   restaurant   French
113 Rempart Augustins   tel. 02 48 54 01 44
http://www.restaurant-traiteur-lesaugustins.com/contact.php
Notes: €€ - €€€

SARAN

Biocoop Orleans Nord   health food store   40 rue Gabriel Debacq

SAUMUR

La Reine de Sicile   restaurant   French
71 rue Waldeck-Rousseau   tel. 02 41 67 30 48
Notes: €€

Just another Chateau (M. Rossi)

L'Auberge Saint Pierre   restaurant   French
6 place St Pierre   tel. 02 41 51 26 25   auberge-saintpierre.com/
Notes: €€

Le Pot Au Lapin   restaurant   French
37 rue Rabelais   tel. 02 41 67 12 86
Notes: €€ - €€€

SAVENAY
Biocoop Le Sillon Bio   health food store
rue des Frétauderies - Centre Cial de la Colleraye

ST MARC SUR MER
Hotel de la Plage   hotel/restaurant   French
37 rue du Commandant-Charcot   tel. 02 40 91 99 01
www.hotel-delaplage.fr
Notes: €€€€. 6 miles southeast of La Baule.

SULLY SUR LOIRE
Le Cafe des Arts   restaurant   French
2 rue du Faubourg Saint-Germain   tel. 02 38 36 20 83 restaurantdesarts.fr/
Notes: €€

Hostellerie Du Grand Sully   hotel/restaurant   French
10 bd du Champ de Foire   tel. 02 38 36 27 56   www.grandsully.com/
Notes: €€€ - €€€€. "Just come."

TOURS

Barju   restaurant   French
15 rue de Change   tel. 02 47 64 91 12   www.barju.fr
Notes: €€€ - €€€€. Advance notice necessary.

La Maison des Halles   restaurant   French
19 place des Halles   tel. 02 47 39 96 90   www.maisondeshalles.com/
Notes: €

La Souris Gourmande   restaurant   French
100 rue Colbert   tel. 02 47 47 04 80   http://lasourisgourmande.com/
Notes: €€. No advance notice necessary. Many celiac clients.

l'Atelier Gourmand   restaurant   French
37 rue Etienne Marcel   tel. 02 47 38 59 87
Notes: €€. Advance notice necessary.

L'Odeon   restaurant   French
10 place Gen Leclerc   tel. 02 47 20 12 65   www.restaurant-lodeon.com
Notes: N/A. No advance notice necessary. Many celiac clients. English spoken.

Salut Terre   health food store   98 rue Georges Méliès

TREBEURDEN

Ti Al Lannec   hotel/restaurant   French
14 allee de Mezo Guen   tel. 02 96 15 01 01   www.tiallannec.com
Notes: €€€€. GF breakfast too. Advance notice.

TRIGNAC

Buffalo Grill   restaurant   French
ZAC de Savine rue des aigrettes RN171   tel. 02 40 90 35 80
www.buffalo-grill.fr
Notes: € - €€. This restaurant chain has a list of foods which are allergen-free and gluten-free.

Les Hameaux Bio Zac   health food store   de Savigne rue des Aigrettes

VALLET
Biocoop La Sangueze   health food store   24 boulevard d'Italie

VIERZON
La Vie Claire   health food store
Centre commercial l'Orée de Sologne - Chemin de l'Ardillat

NORMANDY
(HAUTE-NORMANDIE

AND BASSE-NORMANDIE)

Mont St Michel (L. Diamanti)

ALENCON

La Vie Claire   health food store   3 rue De Lattre De Tassigny

AMFREVILLE LA MIVOIE

Biocoop Du Rouennais   health food store   161 route de Paris

AVRANCHES

Comptoir De La Bio   health food store   16 rue de la Division Leclerc

BAYEUX

La Coline D'Enzo   restaurant   Italian
rue des Bouchers 4   tel. 02 31 92 03 01   www.restaurantbayeux.net
Notes: €€ - €€€

La Rapiere   restaurant   French
53 rue St. Jean   tel. 02 31 21 05 45   http://www.larapiere.net/
Notes: €€€

Le P'tit Resto   restaurant   French
2 rue de Bienvenu   tel. 02 31 51 85 40   www.restaurantbayeux.com
Notes: €€

BOIS-GUILLAUME

Planete Bio   health food store   65 rue Reine des Bois

CAEN

La Mere Michele   restaurant   French
7 rue du Vaugueux   tel. 02 31 93 95 13
Notes: N/A

La Trattoria   restaurant   Italian
13 rue Vaugueux tel. 02 31 47 97 01
Notes: €€€. Many celiac clients.

Le Bouchon du Vaugueux   restaurant   French
12 rue Graindorge   tel. 02 31 44 26 26
Notes: €€€€

Le Carlotta   restaurant   French
16 quai Vendeuvre   tel. 02 31 86 68 99   http://www.lecarlotta.fr/
Notes: €€€

La Vie Claire   health food store   3 rue Basse
Frequence Bio   health food store   Centre Commercial place Venoise

CONNELLES

Moulin de Connelles   Hôtel, restaurant   French
40 route d'Amfreville les Monts   tel. 02 32 59 53 33
Notes: €€€€

COUTANCES

Biocoop Biosaveurs   health food store
rue des Boissières Z.I de l'Auberge de la Mare

DEAUVILLE

Chez Herve   restaurant   French
44 rue Mirabeau   tel. 02 31 87 82 36
Notes: N/A. Many dishes can be made gluten-free.

Le Ciro's Barriere   restaurant   Seafood
Promenade des Planches   tel. 02 31 14 31 31
Notes: €€€ - €€€€

Power Coffee   restaurant   French
11 quai de la Marine 11 quai de Deauville   tel. 02 31 89 31 80
Notes: €

DIEPPE

Planete Bio Dieppe Zac   health food store du Val Druel Ave des Canadiens

ÉTRETAT

Lann-Bihoue   restaurant   French
45 rue Notre-Dame   tel. 02 35 27 04 65   www.lannbihoue.com/
Notes: €. Enjoy their buckwheat galettes!

Le Bicorne   restaurant   French
5 bd President Rene Coty   tel. 02 35 29 62 22   www.hws.fr/lebicorne
Notes: €€ - €€€€

Les Roches Blanches   restaurant   Seafood
rue de l'Abbe-Cochet   tel. 02 35 27 07 34
Notes: €€€

EVREUX

Biocoop Evreux   health food store   1 rue Jacques Monod

American cemetery Normandy (J.Coyne)

FÉCAMP

L'Ardoise   restaurant   French
113 rue des Pres   tel. 02 35 10 99 17
Notes: €€ - €€€

Les Terre Neuvas   restaurant   French
63 Blvd Albert   tel. 02 35 29 22 92   www.lesterreneuvas.com/
Notes: €€ - €€€

FLERS

La Source Verte   health food store   129 rue de la Chaussée

GAP

Le Grenier   health food store   3 rue Alphonse Daudet

GRANVILLE

Biocoop Biosaveurs   health food store   788 ave l'Europe–Yquelon

HEROUVILLE ST CLAIR

Jonathan   health food store   1 ter rue Denis Papin

HONFLEUR

L'Endroit   restaurant   French
3 rue Charles-et-Paul-Breard   tel. 02 31 88 08 43
Notes: €€€. Many dishes can be prepared gluten-free. Many celiac clients

Restaurant Les Deux Ponts   restaurant   French
20 quai de la Quarantaine   tel. 02 31 89 04 37 http://www.lesdeuxponts.fr/
Notes: €€. English spoken. Many celiac clients.

JUANS LES PINS
Biocoop Les Pins   health food store   8 rue Saint Honorat

MONDEVILLE
Leon de Bruxelles   restaurant   Belgian
route de Paris Lotissement L'Etoile   tel. 03 22 46 35 03
www.leon-de-bruxelles.fr
Notes: €€€. This restaurant is part of a large chain all over France. They have limited items that are GF, but their Director of Quality Control nationwide provided us with a list of menu items that are GF. See page 16.

MONT ST-MICHEL
Auberge Saint-Pierre   restaurant, inn   French
BP 16 Grande Rue   tel. 02 33 60 14 03
www.auberge-saint-pierre.fr/restaurant
Notes: €€ - €€€€. Either phone in or e-mail GF request.

La Sirene   restaurant, crêperie   French
Grande Rue   tel. 02 33 60 08 60
Notes: N/A

Ferme St. Michel   restaurant   French
Lieu dit Le bas Pays   tel. 02 33 58 46 79
www.restaurant-ferme-saint-michel.com/
Notes: € - €€

Relais St. Michel   hotel, restaurant   French
La Caserne | BP 31   tel. 02 33 89 32 00   www.relais-st-michel.com
Notes: Must contact ahead of time. Will do dinner and breakfast gluten-free.

ROUEN
Gill Restaurant   restaurant   French
Quai de la Bourse   tel. 02 35 71 16 14   www.gill.fr

La Pecherie   restaurant   Seafood
place Basse Vieille Tour   tel. 02 35 88 71 00   www.lapecherie.fr
Notes: €€€

Chateau des Montgomery in Ducey, Lower Normandy (T. Curtis)

La Petite Bouffe   restaurant   French
rue Eau de Robec   tel. 02 35 98 13 14   http://lapetitebouffe.ifrance.com
Notes: €€. Very amenable to serving gluten-free clients.

Le 37   restaurant   French
37 rue St Etienne des Tonneliers   tel. 02 35 70 56 65   www.le37.fr
Notes: €€. Will serve gluten-free but you need to bring some kind of a celiac
card identifying what it is you can and can't eat. Use the one in the front of
this book.)

Les Ptits Parapluies   restaurant   French
place de la Rougemare   tel. 02 35 88 55 26   www.lesptits-parapluies.com/
Notes: €€€€. Many dishes to choose from.

Restaurant La Couronne   restaurant   French
31 place Vieux Marche   tel. 02 35 71 40 90   www.lacouronne.com.fr
Notes: €€€€

| **La Vie Claire** | health food store | 74 rue Aux Ours |
| **La Vie Claire** | health food store | 23 place St. Marc |

SAINT LO

Buffalo Grill   restaurant   French
Lotissement "Parc Europe"   boulevard de Strasbourg   tel. 02 33 55 04 21
www.buffalo-grill.fr
Notes: € - €€. This restaurant chain has a list of foods which areallergen free and gluten-free.

La Peche Mignon   restaurant   French
84 rue Marechal Juin   tel. 02 33 72 23 77
http://le-peche-mignon.monsite-orange.fr/
Notes: €€

La Pergola   restaurant   Italian
11 rue Villedieu   tel. 02 33 55 17 27
Notes: N/A

TROUVILLE

Brasserie Les Voiles   restaurant   French
162 Quai Fernand Moureaux   tel. 02 31 88 45 85   www.lesvoiles.fr/
Notes: N/A

La Petite Auberge   restaurant   French
7 rue Carnot   tel. 02 31 88 11 07   www.lapetiteaubergesurmer.fr
Notes: €€€

Le Noroit   restaurant   French
118 boulevard Fernand Moureaux   tel. 02 31 81 41 44
Notes: N/A

VERNON

Biocoop Vernon   health food store   10 boulevard Isambard

BRITTANY (BRETAGNE)

Josselin Chateau (T. Curtis)

BELLE ILE EN MER

Castel Clara   hotel/restaurant   French
Port-Goulphar   tel. 02 97 31 84 21   www.castel-clara.com
Notes: €€€

BELZ

Biocoop La Bel'Saison   health food store
rue Gutemberg – Parc d'Activité de la Riad Etel

BREST

Buffalo Grill   restaurant   French
Rond Point Pen Ar C'hleus rue de Keranfurust   tel. 02 98 02 02 72
www.buffalo-grill.fr
Notes: € - €€. This restaurant chain has a list of foods which are allergen-free and gluten-free.

Kerbio Coop	health food store	3 rue Kerfautras
Kerbio Coop Ii	health food store	114 boulevard Plymouth
La Vie Claire	health food store	41 rue Louis Pasteur

CARHAIX

Douar Nevez   health food store   4 rue Charles Le Goff

CARNAC

La Brigantine   restaurant   Seafood
3 rue Colary   tel. 02 97 52 17 72   http://labrigantine.net/
Notes: €€ - €€€. Very nice staff. "Yes of course: just come."

La Calypso   restaurant   Seafood
158 rue du Po   tel. 02 97 52 06 14   www.calypso-carnac.com/
Notes: €€ - €€€

Restaurant La Cote   restaurant   French
Lieu-dit Kermario   tel. 02 97 52 02 80   www.restaurant-la-cote.com
Notes: €€€€

CESSON SEVIGNE

Scarabee Cesson   health food store   12 avenue des Peupliers

DINARD

Chez Ma Pomme   restaurant   French
6 rue Yves Verney   tel. 02 99 46 81 90
Notes: €€ - €€€. Advance notice necessary.

Klem's   restaurant   French
2 rue des Bains   tel. 02 99 46 93 25   www.klems-restaurant.com
Notes: €€. No advance notice necessary.

Le Balafon   restaurant   Bio
31 Vallee   tel. 02 99 46 14 81
Notes: €€€. Advance notice necessary.

DOUARNENEZ
Biocoop Dz   health food store   12 rue Pen ar Nenez

FOUGERES
Biocoop Bio Lune   health food store   32 bd de Groslay

JOSSELIN
Hôtel Restaurant du Château hotel and restaurant   French
1 rue du Général de Gaulle   tel. 02 97 22 20 11
http://www.hotel-chateau.com/
Notes: €€€€

LA RICHARDAIS
Biocoop Emeraude   health food store
Parc d'activité du Haut Chemin, rue Ville Biais

LAMBALLE
Le Courtil Bio   health food store   17 rue Saint-Martin

LANDERNEAU
Biocoop La Clef Des Champs health food store   11 Henri Dunant

LANESTER
Biocoop Les 7 Epis   health food store
87 avenue Ambroize Croizat

LANGUEUX
La Vie Claire   health food store   11 rue Ambroise Paré

LANNION
Douargann   health food store   Rond-Point Saint-Marc
La Vie Claire   health food store   Zone Commerciale Saint Marc
Traou An Douar   health food store   rue J.P Sartre ZAC Kerligonan

LANVALLAY
Biocoop Element Terre health food store   rue Charles de Gaulle

LESNEVEN

Prim'Vert health food store 8 croas ar Rod

LORIENT

Les 7 Epis health food store 5 rue du Colonel Le Barillec Z.I. Keryado

MELLAC

Les 7 Epis Mellac health food store Z.A.C. de Keringant /27 Kervidanou 3

PAIMPOL

La Cotriade restaurant Breton
16 quai Armand Dayot tel. 02 96 20 81 08
http://la-cotriade.com/coteouest.pdf
Notes: €€

PERROS GUIREC

Douar Bihan health food store rue Anatole Le Bras

PLERIN

Biocoop La Ti Gambille health food store rue de la Prunelle

PLOEMEUR

La Vie Claire health food store 5 rue de Larmor

PLOEREN

Buffalo Grill restaurant French
17 rue Edgar Touffreau tel. 02 97 40 63 00 www.buffalo-grill.fr
Notes: € - €€. This restaurant chain has a list of foods which areallergen free
and gluten-free.

PLOERMEL

Biocoop Seve health food store 9 bd des Carmes

PLOUGASTEL

Biogastell health food store 45 rue Fournier

PLOUMAGOAR

Biocoop Guingampaise Zac health food store de Runanvizit

PLOUZANE

Mille et Une Lunes restaurant regional French
5175 route de Minou tel. 02 98 48 41 81
Notes: € - €€. 10min from Brest, on the beach Minou, offers gluten-free
meals.

PONT L'ABBE

Graine De Bio   health food store
route de Plomeur Rond Point de Kerrouant

PONT-AVEN

Le Grain de Ble   restaurant   creperie
46 rue des Abbes Tanguy   tel. 02 98 09 10 88
Notes: €. No advance notice necessary.

Les Ajoncs d'Or Hotel Restaurant hotel/restaurant   French
1 place de l'Hotel de Ville   tel. 02 98 06 02 06
Notes: €€€€. Advance notice necessary. Will serve all three meals GF.

Moulin de Rosmadec   hotel/restaurant   French
Centre Ville   tel. 02 98 06 00 22   www.moulinderosmadec.com
Notes: €€€€. GF breakfast too. Advance notice.

PONTIVY

L'Aiglon   restaurant   French
42 rue Generale de Gaulle   tel. 02 97 27 98 08
http://www.laiglon-pontivy.com
Notes: €€

L'Auberge de L'Ile   restaurant   French
3 rue de la Fontaine   tel. 02 97 25 15 30   www.auberge-de-lile56.com
Notes: € - €€. Variety of gluten free dishes on menu. Staff speaks English

Biocoop Callune health food store   26 avenue De Lattre De Tassigny

QUIMPER

Biocooop Ty Bio   health food store   1 route de Quimper
Biocoop Quimper   health food store   5 Allée de Tréquéffelec

QUINTIN

Hôtel du Commerce   hotel and restaurant   French
2 rue de Rochonen   tel. 02 96 74 94 67
www.hotelducommerce-quintin.com
Notes: €

REDON

Le Heron Bleu   health food store   51 rue de la Châtaigneraie

RENNES

Café Clochette   restaurant   French
37 rue de Dinan   tel. 02 99 35 80 89   www.cafeclochette.com/
Notes: €. Extremely knowledgeable and helpful about GF. Kid-centered café/restaurant.

La Vie Claire   health food store   7 rue Poullain Duparc

ROSTRENEN

L'Eventail   restaurant   French
13 rue Saint-Georges   tel. 02 99 63 44 25
Notes: €€€€

SAINT AVÉ

Le Pressoir   restaurant   French
7 rue Hôpital   tel. 02 97 60 87 63   http://www.le-pressoir.fr/
Notes: €€€€

SAINT BRIEUC

La Gambille   health food store   10 rue de Robien
La Vie Claire   health food store   6/8 rue St Gilles

SAINT GREGOIRE

Scarabee St Gregoire   health food store   8 rue de la Cerisaie

SAINT JOUAN DES GUERETS

La Vie Claire   health food store
rue Siochan Zone d'activité Moulin du domaine

SAINT MALO

Biotea Cook   restaurant   Contemporary, healthy, vegetarian, Deli
8 rue des Cordiers   tel. 02 99 20 08 36 www.restaurant-st-malo-bioteacook
Notes: €€. Many celiac clients. Advance notice.

Café de la Bourse   café   French
1 rue Dinan   tel. 02 99 56 47 17
Notes: €€

La Cale   restaurant   Local French
5 quai Solidor   tel. 02 99 81 99 34
Notes: €€€. Many celiac clients. Prefer three days Advance notice.

Le Café de L'Ouest   restaurant   Seafood, bistro, French
4 place Chateaubriand   tel. 02 99 56 63 49
Notes: €€. No advance notice necessary.

Le Saint Placide   restaurant   French
6 place Poncel   tel. 02 99 81 70 73
Notes: €€€€. Advance notice necessary.

Restaurant Bouche en Folie   restaurant   French
14 rue du Boyer   tel. 06 72 49 08 89   http://boucheenfolie.eresto.net/
Notes: €€€. Many celiac clients. Advance notice necessary.

Biocoop Saint Malo Zac health food store   de la Grassinais
La Vie Claire   health food store   7 place Bouvet

SAINT MARTIN DES CHAMPS
Coccinelle   health food store   65 route de Sainte Sève

SAINTE ANNE LA PALUD
Hotel de la Plage   hotel/restaurant   French
Sainte Anne la Palud   tel. 02 90 92 50 12   www.plage.com
Notes: €€€€. Call ahead.

VANNES
Le Boudoir   restaurant   French
43 rue de la Fontaine   tel. 02 97 42 60 64   www.restaurantleboudoir.com
Notes: €€€. Advance notice necessary.

Regis Mahe   restaurant   Seafood
24 place de la Gare   tel. 02 97 42 61 41
Notes: €€€€. Please give three hours advance notice.

Terroirs   restaurant   gastronomique
22 Fontaine   tel. 02 97 47 57 52   www.terroirs-restaurant.com
Notes: €. Very nice staff. Advance notice necessary.

Kyriad   hotel/restaurant   French
8 place de la Liberation   tel. 02 97 63 27 36   www.kyriad-vannes.fr
Notes: €€

La Vie Claire   health food store   Centre commercial Tohannic

CHAMPAGNE COUNTRY (CHAMPAGNE-ARDENNE)

Sparkles at night (J. Rossi)

AMIENS

Buffalo Grill   restaurant   French
ZAC de la Vallée des Vignes 49 avenue de Grèce   tel. 03 22 95 50 55
www.buffalo-grill.fr
Notes: € - €€. This restaurant chain has a list of foods which are allergen-free
and gluten-free.

Le Bouchon   restaurant   French
10 rue Alexandre Fatton   tel. 03 22 92 14 32   www.lebouchon.fr
Notes: €€ - €€€

Les Marissons   restaurant   French
68 rue des Marissons Pont de la Dodone   tel. 03 22 92 96 66
www.les-marissons.fr
Notes: €€€

Les Marronniers   restaurant   regional French
27 rue Metz   tel. 03 22 91 30 55   www.restaurantlesmarronniers.fr
Notes: € - €€

Biocoop Amiens   health food store   2505 chaussée Jules Ferry
La Vie Claire   health food store   1 bis rue des Chaudronniers

BEAUVAIS

La Table de Celine   restaurant   French
6 bis rue Antoine Caron   tel. 03 44 45 79 79 www.restaurant-beauvais.com
Notes: € - €€

Les Mille Bleuets   restaurant   French
1 route Dangu   tel. 02 32 55 91 99

Les Vents D'anges   restaurant   French
1 place St Etienne   tel. 03 44 15 00 08   www.lesventsdanges.com/
Notes: €

BRIANCON

L'Epine Vinette   health food store
Le Val Chancel bât. A av. du 159è RIA

CHÂLONS-EN-CHAMPAGNE

141   restaurant gastronomique   Italian/French
1 Mar Foch   tel. 03 26 21 48 01
Notes: €€

La Sicilienne   restaurant   Italian
50 rue Grande Etape   tel. 03 26 68 54 51
Notes: €€ - €€€

Biocoop Initiative Bio   health food store   17 ave du Général Sarrail
La Vie Claire   health food store   23 place Godart

CHARLEVILLE MEZIERES
La Vie Claire   health food store   17 place de Nevers

CHÂTEAU-THIERRY
Il Calcio   restaurant   Italian
5 Hotel de Ville   tel. 03 23 69 11 11
Notes: N/A. Some English spoken.

La Vie Claire   health food store   4 place l'Hôtel de Ville

ÉPERNAY
La banque formules Brasserie   restaurant   French
40 rue du General Leclerc   tel. 03 26 59 50 50 www.brasserie-labanque.fr
Notes: € - €€

Le Vieux Puits   restaurant   French
18 rue Roger Sondag   tel. 03 26 56 96 53
Notes: N/A

Les Berceaux   restaurant   French
13 rue des Berceaux   tel. 03 26 55 28 84
www.lesberceaux.com/restaurant.htm
Notes: €€€€

LAON
La Gourmandine   restaurant   French
16 avenue Carnot   tel. 03 23 23 22 40   www.lagourmandine-laon.com
Notes: N/A. With advance notice will purchase gluten-free foodstuffs to prepare.

Bonniere de France   hotel, restaurant   French
11 rue Franklin Roosevelt   tel. 03 23 23 21 44
www.hoteldelabannieredefrance.com
Notes: €. English spoken. Will serve breakfast and dinner gluten-free.

L'EPINE

Aux Armes de Champagne   hotel, restaurant   French
31 avenue du Luxembourg   tel. 03 26 69 30 25
http://www.aux-armes-de-champagne.com/
Notes: €€€€

REIMS

Le Foch   restaurant   French
34 boulevard Foch   tel. 03 26 47 48 22   http://www.lefoch.com/
Notes: €€€. Many celiac customers.

Le Grand Café   restaurant   French
92 place Drouet d'Erlon   tel. 03 26 47 61 50   www.le-grandcafe.com
Notes: €€€€

Version Originale   restaurant   International
25 bis rue du Temple   tel. 03 26 02 69 32   www.vo-reims.fr
Notes: €€€

Chateau Les Crayeres   hotel, restaurant, brasserie   French
64 bd Henry Vasnier   tel. 03 26 82 80 80   www.lescrayeres.fr
Notes: €€€ - €€€€. Very highly recommended. Extremely willing to make gluten-free breads, breakfast dinners, everything. Must call ahead.

SAINT DIZIER

Les Jardins Naturels health food store   79 avenue Alsace Lorraine

SEPT-SAULX

Le Cheval Blanc   restaurant   French
rue du Moulon   tel. 03 26 03 90 27 www.chevalblanc-sept-saulx.com
Notes: €€€€

SOISSONS

La Cavea   restaurant   French
1 rue Petrot Labarre   tel. 03 23 93 02 01
http://leclubdesbonsvivants.com/restaurant/Picardie/Aisne/Soissons/0210358
5/Cavea-La/Cavea-La.0.html
Notes: €€

La Landolina   restaurant   Italian
16 Pot d'Etain   tel. 03 23 93 22 92
Notes: N/A

Au Panier Naturel   health food store   23 avenue de Compiègne

THILLOIS

Leon de Bruxelles   restaurant   Belgian
Parc Millesime RN 51   tel. 02 38 64 17 11 www.leon-de-bruxelles.fr
Notes: €€€. This restaurant is part of a large chain all over France. They have
limited items that are GF, but their Director of Quality Control nationwide
provided us with a list of menu items that are GF. See page 16.

TINQUEUX

La Bohême   restaurant   Portuguese
83 avenue du 29-août-1944   tel. 03 26 83 93 32
Notes: €

TROYES

La Vie Claire   health food store
Halles de l'Hôtel de Ville 1er étage

VILLECHETIF

Leon de Bruxelles   restaurant   Belgian
2 rue des Vignes ZAC les Mercieres   tel. 03 21 75 63 26
www.leon-de-bruxelles.fr
Notes: €€€. This restaurant is part of a large chain all over France. They have
limited items that are GF, but their Director of Quality Control nationwide
provided us with a list of menu items that are GF. See page 16.

ALSACE-LORRAINE

Tres belle (J. Friedman)

BAINS LES BAINS

Hôtel-Restaurant des Sources   hotel, restaurant   French
place du Bain Romain   tel. 03 29 36 30 23
Notes: €

BARR

Aux saisons gourmandes   restaurant   French
23 rue de la Kirneck   tel. 03 88 08 12 77   www.saisons-gourmandes.com/
Notes: € - €€. The restaurant is small and reservations are an absolute must.

Hotel Restaurant du Chateau d'Andlau   restaurant   French
113 rue de la Vallee   tel. 03 88 08 96 78   www.hotelchateauandlau.fr
Notes: €€ - €€€. There is a lot to choose from that can be made GF.

COLMAR

La Taverne Alsacienne   restaurant   French
9 rue de la Republique   tel. 03 89 27 08 41
Notes: €€€€. Many celiac clients and many GF choices.

Maison Rouge   restaurant   French
9 rue des Ecoles   tel. 03 89 23 53 22   www.maison-rouge.net/
Notes: €€

Palmyre   restaurant   French
1 rue Canard   tel. 03 89 41 57 13
Notes: N/A

Wistub de la Petite Venise   restaurant   French
4 rue Poissonnerie   tel. 03 89 41 72 59
Notes: €€ - €€€. Will only make GF food if you call ahead of time.

Sonnebluem   health food store   7 rue du Grillenbreit

DAMBACH-LA-VILLE

Restaurant Schwarzbach   hotel/restaurant   French
18 route De Sturzelbronn | Dambach-Neunhoffen   tel. 03 88 09 20 44
http://rest.schwarzbach.free.fr
Notes: €€. Advance notice necessary.

DOMREMY

Accueil du Pelerin   restaurant   French
2 La Basilique   tel. 03 29 94 14 38
Notes: N/A

ÉPINAL

Brasserie du Commerce   restaurant   French
15 place des Vosges Le Commerce Hotel   tel. 03 29 34 21 65
Notes: N/A. Advance notice necessary.

ESSEY LES NANCY

Leon de Bruxelles   restaurant   Belgian
74 route Nationale   tel. 04 73 14 05 94   www.leon-de-bruxelles.fr
Notes: €€€. This restaurant is part of a large chain all over France. They have
limited items that are GF, but their Director of Quality Control nationwide
provided us with a list of menu items that are GF. See page 16.

Leon de Bruxelles   restaurant   Belgian
5 rue de la Pallée   tel. 04 67 99 91 46   www.leon-de-bruxelles.fr
Notes: €€€. This restaurant is part of a large chain all over France. They have
limited items that are GF, but their Director of Quality Control nationwide
provided us with a list of menu items that are GF. See page 16.

INGERSHEIM

Unis Vers Bio   health food store   36 route d'Eguisheim

JOUY AUX ARCHES

La Vie Saine   restaurant   Bio
Allée des Tilleuls - ZAC Actisud   tel. 03 87 62 94 80
http://www.guide-restaurant-bio.com/restaurants-jouy-aux-arches/restaurant-
bio-la-vie-saine,458.php
Notes: €

KLINGENTHAL

Restaurant l'Etoile   restaurant   French
7 place de l'Etoile   tel. 03 88 95 82 90
Notes: N/A

METZ

Mougel Bio Gourmand   health food store   53 rue de Haute Seille

METZ SEMECOURT

Leon de Bruxelles   restaurant   Belgian
Lieudit « le patural de la Maxe »   tel. 04 72 05 75 06
www.leon-de-bruxelles.fr
Notes: €€€. This restaurant is part of a large chain all over France. They have
limited items that are GF, but their Director of Quality Control nationwide
provided us with a list of menu items that are GF. See page 16.

MUNSTER

Restaurant Pizzeria Dolce Vita   restaurant   Italian
2 rue des Corbeaux   tel. 03 89 77 12 51   www.dolcevitamunster.fr
 Notes: €

NANCY

A La Table du Bon Roi Stanislas   restaurant   French/Polish
7 rue Gustave Simon | Ville Vieille/Stanislas   tel. 03 83 35 36 52
http://tablestan.free.fr/
Notes: €€ - €€€. Must give 24hr notice for GF.

Grand Cafe Foy   restaurant   French, gastropub
1 place Stanislas   tel. 03 83 32 15 97
Notes: €€€. Just tell what you can and can't eat.

Les funambules   restaurant   French
30 place des Vosges   tel. 03 83 18 33 02
Notes: €-€€€. Chef is very familiar with gluten intolerance.

L'Excelsior   restaurant   French
50 rue Henri-Poincare   tel. 03 83 35 24 57   www.brasserie-excelsior.com
Notes: €€

Restaurant Les Agaves Cote Sud   restaurant   French
2 rue Carmes   tel. 03 83 32 14 14
Notes: €€ - €€€

Le Goupil Vert   health food store   34/38 rue Marcel Brot

OBERHOFFEN SUR MODER

La Vie Claire   health food store
rue du Commerce

OBERNAI

Cinecitta   restaurant   Italian
1 rue Gen Leclerc   tel. 03 88 48 31 31
Notes: N/A

Les Petites Casseroles   restaurant   French vegetarian
128 rue du General Gouraud   tel. 03 88 04 70 21
www.casserole-obernai.com/
Notes: €. Vegetarian restaurant

Les Remparts d'Obernai   restaurant   French
3 Marche   tel. 03 88 95 15 52
Notes: N/A

OSTWALD
La Vie Claire   health food store   52 rue du Général Leclerc

PLOBSHEIM
Restaurant Au Boeuf   restaurant   French
25 rue du Generél Leclerc   tel. 03 88 98 58 25   www.restaurantauboeuf.fr/
Notes: N/A

PULNOY
La Vie Claire   health food store   2 rte de Tarbes Prolongées

RIBEAUVILLÉ
Hotel – Restaurant du Mouton   restaurant   French
5 place de la Sinne   tel. 03 89 73 60 11   www.hoteldumouton.fr
Notes: €€

Zum   restaurant   German
14 Grand Rue   tel. 03 89 73 62 28
Notes: €

RIQUEWIHR
D'Brendel Stub   restaurant   French
48 rue Gen de Gaulle   tel. 03 89 86 54 54
Notes: €€ - €€€. "No problem!" There are many choices for GF dining.

La Grenouille   restaurant   French
7 rue Couronne   tel. 03 89 86 01 12
Notes: €€ - €€€

Le Sarment d'Or   restaurant   French
4 rue du Cerf (in Hotel Le Le Sarment d'Or)   tel. 03 89 86 02 86
Notes: €. "No problem!" Ask for gluten-free when you make a reservation.

SAINT AMARIN
La Vie Claire   health food store   2 rue Curiale

SAINT DIE
Biocoop La Ciboulette   health food store 21 rue St Exupéry ZC d'Hellieule

SÉLESTAT

Abbaye de la Pommeraie   restaurant   French
8 Blvd du Marechal Foch   tel. 03 88 92 07 84   www.pommeraie.fr/
Notes: €€€

Restaurant Le Rosti Huus   restaurant   French
4 rue Cerf   tel. 03 88 92 90 43
Notes: N/A. Many celiac clients.

A La Belle Epoque   hotel, restaurant   French
place du Marche au Choux   tel. 03 88 92 15 43 www.a-la-belle-epoque.fr
Notes: €€

G'Sundheit   health food store   19 rue du Sel

SERRES

L'Épicerie Bio   health food store   7 av. Marius Méyère

STRASBOURG

Au Crocodile   restaurant   French contemporary
10 rue de l'Outre   tel. 03 88 32 13 02
Notes: €€€€

Chez Nous   restaurant   French
3 rue Puits   tel. 03 88 14 04 31
Notes: N/A

Chez Yvonne   restaurant   French
10 rue du Sanglier   tel. 03 88 32 84 15   www.chez-yvonne.net
Notes: €

Ecrin des Saveurs   restaurant   French
5 rie Leitersperger   tel. 03 88 39 21 20   http://www.ecrinsaveurs.com/
Notes: €€€€

Goh restaurant   restaurant   French
4 place St-Pierre Le jeune | Hotel Sofitel Grande Ile   tel. 03 88 15 49 10
www.goh-restaurant.com
Notes: €€€

La Table du Chef   restaurant   French traditional and new
1 avenue Herrenschmidt   tel. 03 88 37 10 10   http://www.hilton.com
Notes: €€€€. Located in Hilton Hotel. Will serve GF with advance notice.

Le Buerehiesel   restaurant   French
4 parc de l'Orangerie   tel. 03 88 45 56 65   www.buerehiesel.fr
Notes: €€€

Le Clou   restaurant   Alsace
3 rue Chaudron   tel. 03 88 32 11 67   http://www.le-clou.com/
Notes: €€ - €€€

Le Gavroche   restaurant   French
4 rue Klein   tel. 03 88 36 82 89   www.restaurant-gavroche.com/
Notes: N/A

Le Jardin du Tivoli   restaurant   French
1 avenue Herrenschmidt   tel. 03 88 37 10 10   http://www.hilton.com
Notes: €€€. Located in Hilton Hotel. Will serve GF with advance notice.

Maison Kammerzell   restaurant   French
16 place de la Cathedrale   tel. 03 88 32 42 14
www.maison-kammerzell.com
Notes: €€

Poêles de carottes   restaurant   bio/vegetarian
2 place des Meuniers   tel. 03 88 32 33 23   www.poelesdecarottes.com
Notes: €€€€. GF items marked on menu.

Hilton Strasbourg hotel hotel with two restaurants   French
1 avenue Herrenschmidt   tel. 03 88 37 10 10   www.clubmed.com
Notes: €€€€. Will serve GF room service with Advance notice. Also has a
restaurant.

VANDOEUVRE LES NANCY
Leon de Bruxelles   restaurant   Belgian
7 rue d'Albertville   tel. 04 77 90 22 69   www.leon-de-bruxelles.fr
Notes: €€€. This restaurant is part of a large chain all over France. They have
limited items that are GF, but their Director of Quality Control nationwide
provided us with a list of menu items that are GF. See page 16.

VITTEL
Club Med Vittel Ermitage all-inclusive resort   French
tel. 03 29 08 81 50   http://www.clubmed.com
Notes: €€€€

Club Med Vittel Le Parc   all-inclusive resort   French
tel. 03 29 08 18 80   http://www.clubmed.com
Notes: €€€€

XONRUPT LONGEMER

Auberge du Lac   restaurant   French
2887 route de Colmar   tel. 03 29 63 37 21
Notes: €€€€

Hôtel-Restaurant des Lacs   hotel, restaurant   French
route des Lacs
Notes: €€€€

BURGUNDY
(BOURGOGNE)

Chateau Nozet (X. EDos)

ANNONAY

Bionacelle health food store rue Sadi Carnot

AUTUN

Le Relais de Dettey restaurant French
Le Bourg | Dettey tel. 03 85 54 57 19
Notes: N/A. Advance notice. Just a chef dietary needs.

Les Ursulines restaurant French
14 rue Rivault tel. 03 85 86 58 58
Notes: € - €€

Restaurant le Chapitre restaurant French
13 place du Terreau tel. 03 85 52 04 01 www.restaurantlechapitre.com
Notes: €€. Advance notice for GF is preferable.

La Vie Claire health food store 37 place du Champes De Mars

AUXERRE

La Cuisine Au Vin Chablis restaurant French
16 rue Auxerroise tel. 03 86 18 98 52
Notes: €. Reservations are preferred but not essential.

La Salamandre restaurant French
84 rue Paris tel. 03 86 52 87 87 www.lasalamandre-auxerre.fr
Notes: €€€ - €€€€. Reservations are essential. They can do many gluten-free dishes.

Le Jardin Gourmand restaurant French
56 boulevard Vauban tel. 03 86 51 53 52 www.lejardingourmand.com
Notes: €€€€. Reservations are an absolute must.

Le Maxime restaurant French
5 Quai de la Marine tel. 03 86 52 04 41 www.lemaxime.fr
Notes: €€ - €€€. Reservations are an absolute must.

La Vie Claire health food store
avenue de Worms Zone des Clairions

Germinal health food store 22 rue de Preuilly

AVALLON

La Vie Claire health food store 9 rue de Paris

BEAUNE

Caveau des Arches   restaurant   French
10 bd Perpreuil   tel. 03 80 22 10 37
http://www.caveau-des-arches.com/restaurant-beaune/en/the-menu-restaurant-in-beaune.html
Notes: €€. "Of course!". Advance notice required.

Le Cheval Noir   restaurant   French
17 bd St Jacques   tel. 03 80 22 07 37   www.restaurant-lechevalnoir.fr/
Notes: €€. Very good choice for gluten-free food. Advance notice.

Le Jardin des Remparts   restaurant   French
10 rue de l'Hotel Dieu   tel. 03 80 24 79 41
www.le-jardin-des-remparts.com
Notes: €€€. Will serve gluten-free food "with pleasure". Advance notice
necessary.

L'Ecusson Restaurant   restaurant   French
2 rue Lieut Dupuis   tel. 03 80 24 03 82   www.ecusson.fr
Notes: €€€

La Vie Claire   health food store   32/34 place Madeleine

CLOS DE VOUGEOT

Côté Terroirs   restaurant   French
Gilly-les-Citeaux in hotel Chateau de Gilly   tel. 03 80 62 89 98
http://www.grandesetapes.fr/fr/Chateau-hotel-gilly/
Notes: €€€€. E-mail in advance to gilly@grandesetapes.fr

Chateau de Gilly   hotel, restaurant   French
Gilly-les-Citeaux   tel. 03 80 62 89 98
http://www.grandesetapes.fr/fr/Chateau-hotel-gilly/
Notes: €€€ - €€€€. Hotel with two restaurants. Will serve all meals gluten-free. E-mail in advance to gilly@grandesetapes.fr.

Le Clos Prieur   restaurant   French
Gilly-les-Citeaux in hotel Chateau de Gilly   tel. 03 80 62 89 98
http://www.grandesetapes.fr/fr/Chateau-hotel-gilly/
Notes: €€€€. E-mail in advance to gilly@grandesetapes.fr

COSNE SUR LOIRE

La Vie Claire   health food store   30 rue du Marechal Leclerc

DIJON

Au Bon Pantagruel   restaurant   French
20 rue Quentin   tel. 03 80 30 68 69
Notes: €€€

Enfaim c'bio   restaurant   Bio/vegetarian
7 boulevard de la Tremouille   tel. 03 80 71 60 05 chrisdusart.perso.sfr.fr
Notes: €€€ - €€€€

La Dame d'Aquitaine   restaurant   French
23 place Bossuet   tel. 03 80 30 45 65
www.ladamedaquitaine.fr/index2.html
Notes: €€€€. Please call the day that you are coming to notify the chef.

Le Pre aux Clercs   restaurant   French
13 place de la Liberation   tel. 03 80 38 05 05   www.jeanpierrebilloux.com
Notes: €€€€. Reservations absolutely essential.

L'Epicerie & Cie   restaurant   French
5 place Emile Zola   tel. 03 80 30 70 69   www.lepicerie-dijon.fr/
Notes: €

L'Escargot   restaurant   French
43 rue Jean Jacques Rousseau   tel. 03 80 73 33 85
http://www.restaurantlescargot-dijon.com/
Notes: € - €€

Stephane Derbord   restaurant   French
10 place Wilson   tel. 03 80 67 74 64   www.restaurantstephanederbord.fr
Notes: €€€€

Antidotes	health food store	11 rue de Bellevue
La Vie Claire	health food store	6 rue Pasteur
Terres Bio	health food store	126 route d'Ahuy

DOLE

Reponse Nature   health food store   65 avenue Eisenhower

ETIVEY

Aux Biscuits d'Antoine   GF bakery   French
5 Petite Rue   tel. 03 86 55 71 73   http://biscuits-antoine.com/
Notes: N/A

JOIGNY

La Vie Claire   health food store   40 avenue Gambetta

MACON

La Vie Claire   health food store   94 route de Lyon

MONTCEAU LES MINES

La Vie Claire   health food store   4 rue Paul Bert

NEVERS

Biocoop Nevers   health food store   32 rue des Grands Jardins

NUITS-ST-GEORGES

La Cabotte   restaurant   French
24 Grande Rue   tel. 03 80 61 20 77   www.lacabotte.com
Notes: €€€€. Advance notice.

La Toute Petite Auberge   restaurant   French
R.N 74 Vosne-Romanee   tel. 03 80 61 02 03
Notes: €. Reservations essential.

QUETIGNY

Biocoop Terres Bio Quetigny health food store   1 rue des Ciseaux

SAULIEU

La Borne Imperiale   restaurant   French
16 rue d'Argentine   tel. 03 80 64 19 76
http://www.borne-imperiale.com/restaurant
Notes: €€

Les Belles Heures Du Cafe Parisien restaurant   French
4 Marche   tel. 03 80 64 26 56
Notes: €€

Hotel de La Poste   hotel, restaurant   French
1 rue Grillot   tel. 03 80 64 05 67
Notes: €€€€. They can also serve a gluten-free breakfast.

SENS

La cuisine de Lolie   restaurant   World cuisine
75 Grande Rue   tel. 03 86 88 43 51   www.lacuisinedelolie.fr
Notes: €€€

| **Germinal** | health food store | 1 rue du Pont de Fer |

TONNERRE

| **Germinal** | health food store | 15 bis bd Georges Lemoine |

TOURNUS

| **La Vie Claire** | health food store | 33 rue de la République |

TROYES

La Maree restaurant French
Espace Cine City | 14 rue des Bas Trévois tel. 03 25 46 23 84
www.troyesenchampagne.com
Notes: €€€

Le Bistroquet restaurant French
10 rue Louis Ulbach tel. 03 25 73 65 65 www.bistroquet-troyes.fr
Notes: €. Very willing to make gluten-free food.

Le Bon Vivent restaurant French fusion
rue Turenne tel. 03 25 73 23 66 www.lebonvivent.com
Notes: €

Le Cafe de l'Union restaurant French
34 rue Champeaux tel. 03 25 40 35 76
Notes: N/A

VALLON PONT D'ARC

Biocoop La Maison Du Bio health food store
Quartier Le Grand Jardin / route de Ruoms

VÉZELAY

Hotel de La Poste et du Lion restaurant French
place du Champ-de-Foire tel. 03 86 33 21 23 www.laposte-liondor.com
Notes: €€ - €€€. GF dinner and breakfast.

Le Bourgainville restaurant French
26 rue St Etienne tel. 03 86 33 27 57
Notes: € - €€

LYON AND THE RHONE-ALPS
(RHÔNE-ALPES)

Le Restaurant Paul Bocouse (R. Levy)

AIX-LES-BAINS

Aux Saveurs du Liban   restaurant   Lebanese
25 avenue Grand Port   tel. 04 79 34 29 71   www.saveursduliban.com
Notes: €. Advance notice necessary. Many dishes that can be made GF.

La Rotonde   restaurant   French
7 Square Jean Moulin   tel. 04 79 35 00 60   www.rotonde-aixlesbains.com
Notes: € - €€

Restaurant le 59   restaurant   French
59 rue du Casino   tel. 04 79 88 29 75
www.boris-campanella.fr/restaurant-le-59
Notes: €€€ - €€€€

Restaurant L'Ecuelle   restaurant   French
5 rue Albert 1er   tel. 04 79 35 26 64
Notes: €€ - €€€

ANNECY

F.M.R Le Garcin   restaurant   French
11 rue Paquier   tel. 04 50 45 20 94
Notes: N/A. "Yes of course we can do gluten-free dishes!"

La Ciboulette   restaurant   French
10 rue vaugelas | Cour du Pré Carré   tel. 04 50 45 74 57
www.laciboulette-annecy.com
Notes: €€€ - €€€€. "Yes of course we can do gluten-free dishes!"

Le Freti   restaurant   French
12 rue Sainte Claire-vieille ville   tel. 04 50 51 29 52 lefreti.com
Notes: €€ - €€€. "Yes of course we can do gluten-free dishes!"

L'Heure Bio   restaurant   bio
8 Passage des Bains   tel. 04 50 09 12 43   www.lheurebio.net
Notes: N/A. Frequent GF customers.

Restaurant L'Etage   restaurant   French
13 rue du Paquier   tel. 04 50 51 03 28   www.letageannecy.fr
Notes: €€

Aquarius   health food store   6 rue du 11ème BCA

ANNECY-LE-VIEUX

Canopy   restaurant   bio/vegetarian
10 allée des Tilleuls   tel. 04 50 09 88 08   canopy-zeresto.com
Notes: €€ - €€€. The chef's family is gluten intolerant.

BOURG ST MAURICE

Chillchalet   catered chalet   French
tel. (44) 02078310707   www.chillchalet.com
Notes: €. English spoken!

BOURG-EN-BRESSE

le Francais   restaurant   French
7 av Alsace Lorraine   tel. 04 74 22 55 14
brasserielefrancais.com/bourg_en_bresse/index.php
Notes: N/A. Can do many GF dishes.

Le Bressan   restaurant   French
34 rue de la Republique   tel. 04 74 23 55 24
Notes: €€

Mets et Vins   restaurant   French
11 rue de la Republique   tel. 04 74 45 20 78   www.labalance.fr
Notes: €€

La Vie Claire   health food store   8A Bd Edouard Herriot

BOUVESSE-QUIRIEU

La Reine des Prés   B&B/restaurant   French
Hoai-Linh et Laurent Lefébure Enieu ou Egnieu)   tel. 04 74 83 40 73
http://www.lareinedespres.com
Notes: €€ - €€€

CHAMBÉRY

La Gondola   restaurant   Italian
square Jacques Lovie   tel. 04 79 60 86 70
Notes: €€

La Grange   restaurant   French
33 place Monge   tel. 04 79 85 60 31   www.restaurantlagrange.com
Notes: €€. Many gluten-free options.

Biocoop Casabio Chambery health food store   26 quai de la Rize
Biocoop Casabio Faubourg Mache health food store 106 Faubourg Maché

CHAMONIX-MONT-BLANC

L'Impossibile   restaurant bio   Vegetarian
9 Chemin Cry | route des Pelerins   tel. 04 50 53 20 36
www.restaurant-impossible.com
Notes: €-€€€. Many many gluten-free options.

Casa Valerio   restaurant   Italian
88 rue du Liret   tel. 04 50 55 93 40   www.casavalerio.net
Notes: € - €€

Restaurant Les Jardins   restaurant   French
62 allee du Majestic   tel. 04 50 53 05 64
www.hotelmontblancchamonix.com
Notes: €€€€

Club Med   Resort/restaurant   French
www.clubmed.com/cm/jsp/clubmed_welcome.jsp
Notes: €€€€

CHASSIERS

Le Mas des Faïsses   hotel/B&B/restaurant farmhouse   French
tel. 04 75 88 34 51   www.masdesfaisses.com
Notes: N/A. well-versed in GF diet

CHAZELLES SUR LYON

Le Chou Ravi   health food store   rue de l'Egalité

CLUSES

Croq'Nature   health food store   671 ave Clémenceau

CRAN GEVRIER

La Vie Claire   health food store   16 rue de la Poterie

DRUMETTAZ

Biocoop Aix Les Bains   health food store   74 chemin du Martinet

EVIAN LES BAINS

Cannelle Restaurant   restaurant   French
Quai Paul Leger   tel. 04 50 85 60 10   www.hilton.uk
Notes: €€€€. Located in Hilton Hotel. Will serve GF with advance notice.

Riva Restaurant Bar & Lounge   restaurant   French
Quai Paul Leger   tel. 04 50 85 60 10   www.hilton.uk
Notes: €€€€. Located in Hilton Hotel. Will serve GF with advance notice.

Hilton Evian-les-Bains hotel   hotel with two restaurants   French
Quai Paul Leger   tel. 04 50 84 60 00   www.hilton.uk
Notes: €€€€. Will serve GF room service with advance notice.

GRENOBLE

Au Clair de Lune   restaurant bio   bio
54 rue Très-Cloîtres   tel. 04 76 24 61 17
Notes: €

Auberge napoleon   restaurant   French
7 rue Montorge   tel. 04 76 87 53 64
Notes: €€€€

La Palestria   restaurant   Italian
rue Beyle-Stendhal   tel. 04 76 85 09 15
Notes: € - €€

Biocoop Malherbes	health food store	114 avenue Jean Perrot
Casabio	health food store	32 rue Nicolas Chorier
Casabio 2	health food store	214 cours de la Libération
La Vie Claire	health food store	Zone artisanale Gloriette

GRESY SUR AIX
Biocoop Gresy Sur Aix   health food store   6 rue Boucher de la Ruppelle

LA ROCHE SUR FORON
Aquarius La Roche   health food store   2 rue Perrine

LYON
Blue Elephant Restaurant   restaurant   Thai
70 Quai Charles De Gaulle   tel. 04 78 17 50 50
http://www.hilton.co.uk
Notes: €€€€. Located in Hilton Hotel. Will serve GF with advance notice.

La Brasserie restaurant   restaurant   French brasserie
70 Quai Charles De Gaulle   tel. 04 78 17 50 50
http://www.hilton.co.uk
Notes: €€€€. Located in Hilton Hotel. Will serve GF with advance notice.

Le Jardin intérieur   restaurant   bio
1 rue Justin Godart   tel. 04 72 00 03 02 http://jardininterieur.over-blog.com
Notes: €. Every day they have specific items on the menu that are gluten-free
and dairy free.

Le Shalimar   restaurant   Indian
39 quai Docteur Gailleton   tel. 04 78 42 18 20   www.leshalimar.com/
Notes: €€€

Paul Bocuse, Auberge du Pont   restaurant   French
40 rue de la Plage Collonges au Mont D'Or   tel. 04 7242 9090
www.bocuse.fr/accueil.aspx
Notes: €€€€

Restaurant Aux Trois Gaules   restaurant   Mediterrean
10 rue Burdeau   tel. 04 72 87 08 25
Notes: €

Soline   restaurant   bio/vergetarian
89 rue Paul Bert   tel. 04 78 60 40 43   www.soline.net
Notes: €. Daily dish and dessert without gluten.

Toutes les Couleurs   restaurant   bio
26 cours Imbert Colomès; Mo Croix-Paquet)   tel. 04 72 00 03 95
http://www.touteslescouleurs.fr/
Notes: € - €€

Julia Child mural on wall of the restaurant Paul Bocuse (R. Levy)

Une Cuisine Pour Deux   restaurant   French
8 rue Garet   tel. 04 78 27 87 56
Notes: € - €€

Hilton Lyon hotel   hotel with two restaurants   French
70 Quai Charles De Gaulle   tel. 04 78 17 50 50   www.hilton.co.uk
Notes: €€€€. GF room service with advance notice. Also has a restaurant.

Biocoop Lyon Bellecour   health food store   32 rue du Plat

LYON MEYZIEU

Leon de Bruxelles   restaurant   Belgian
rue du 24 Avril 1915   tel. 03 25 46 22 01   www.leon-de-bruxelles.fr
Notes: €€€. This restaurant is part of a large chain all over France. They have
limited items that are GF, but their Director of Quality Control nationwide
provided us with a list of menu items that are GF. See page 16.

MEGÈVE

Flocons Village   restaurant   Bistro
74 rue St. François   tel. 04 50 78 35 01   www.floconsdesel.com
Notes: €€€€

Le Flocon de Sel   restaurant   French
1175 route de Leutaz   tel. 04 50 21 49 99   www.floconsdesel.com
Notes: €€€€

L'Indochine aux Caves de Megeve   restaurant   Asian
18 rue Ambroise Martin   tel. 04 50 21 30 11
Notes: N/A. Very willing to make GF dishes.

MEYLAN

La Balade des Joyeux Marmitons   restaurant   bio/vegetarian
18 rue des Aiguinards   tel. 04 76 61 90 84 www.labaladedesmarmitons.com
Notes: €. Frequent GF customers.

MODANE

L'Esprit Vert   health food store   22 avenue Jean Jaurès

PÉROUGES

L'Hostellerie de Perouges   Inn, restaurant   French
place du Tilleul   tel. 04 74 61 00 88   www.hostelleriedeperouges.com/
Notes: €€€ - €€€€. With advance notice they can make both dinner and
breakfast gluten-free.

Cour des Lys hotel, restaurant French
17 rue de Lyon   tel. 04 74 61 06 78   www.la-cour-des-lys.com/
Notes: €€€ - €€€€

PORTES LES VALENCE
La Ferme Bio Margerie Portes   health food store
V route de Beauvallon l'Olagnier D°GAP (D111)

PRINGY
Aquarius Pringy   health food store   95 route d'Annecy

ROMANS
Ferme Bio Margerie Romans   health food store   Zone des Chasses

SAINT-DIDIER-SOUS-AUBENAS
Les Gatobio   health food store   960 route de Montélimar

SAINT-EGREVE
Biocoop Casabio Saint-Egreve   health food store 22 avenue de l'Ile Brune

SAINT GERVAIS LES BAINS
La Ferme de Cupelin   restaurant   French
198 route du Château   tel. 04 50 93 47 30   www.ferme-de-cupelin.com
Notes: €€€. Bio restaurant but not necessarily vegetarian. No menu. With advance notice will design dishes that are GF.

SAINT-PERAY
Bar-restaurant rapide du magasin Satoriz   restaurant   French
Zone du Muret   tel. 04 75 78 31 10
Notes: €. Open 12-130.

ST GENEST
Leon de Bruxelles   restaurant   Belgian
rue Jules Vernes Zone d'activité du Tissot   tel. 05 56 07 64 78
www.leon-de-bruxelles.fr
Notes: €€€. This restaurant is part of a large chain all over France. They have limited items that are GF, but their Director of Quality Control nationwide provided us with a list of menu items that are GF. See page 16.

ST-JEAN-DE-MAURIENNE
Label Nature   health food store Z.I. Pré de la Garde 133 avenue d'Italie

TASSIN LA DEMI LUNE
Bioplaisir Ouest   health food store   142 av. Charles de Gaulle

TOURNON-SUR-RHÔNE

Le Farfadet　　　　　　　restaurant　　　　　French
14 place St. Julien　tel. 04 75 08 53 03
http://restaurant-le-farfadet.webliberte.net/
Notes: €€

Michel Chabran　　　　　inn, restaurant　　　French
29 av. du 45e Parallele　tel. 04 75 84 60 09
www.chateauxhotels.com/chabran
Notes: €€€€. Can make a gluten-free breakfast and dinner. No lunch.

VALENCE

Bistrot Des Clercs House of Napoleon Bonaparte restaurant　French
48 rue Grande rue　tel. 04 75 55 55 15
Notes: €€€ - €€€€

Chez Grand Mere　　　　restaurant　　　　　French
3 place Pierre　　tel. 04 75 62 09 90
Notes: €€

PIC　　　　　　　hotel, restaurant, café　French
285 Ave. Victor Hugo　tel. 04 75 44 15 32　www.pic-valence.com
Notes: €€€€. Top-rated, but extremely expensive.there is also a café which is
less expensive.

VILLARS

Le Baraban Za　　　health food store　　　　La Goutte

VILLEURBANNE

Couleurs des mets　　　　restaurant　　　bio/vegetarian
5 rue Alexandre Bouttin　tel. 04 78 84 65 28　www.couleursdesmets.net
Notes: €. GF dishes every day.

Bio Gone　　　　health food store　　　31 rue Gervais Buissière

VOIRON

Bioasis　　　　health food store　　　39 bd de la République

Annecy (J. Friedman)

PROVENCE (PROVENCE-ALPES) AND THE FRENCH RIVIERA (CÔTE D'AZUR)

St Tropez (D.Martin)

AIGUES-MORTES

restaurant   French

4 66 53 93 95

Le Dit-Vin   restaurant   modern French
6 rue du 4 septembre   tel. 04 66 53 52 76   http://www.restoleditvin.com
Notes: €€

Restaurant le "S"   restaurant   modern French
38 rue de la Republique   tel. 04 66 53 74 60   http://le-s.fr/
Notes: €€€

AIX EN PROVENCE

Café La Chimere   restaurant   French
15 rue Brueys   tel. 04 42 38 30 00
Notes: €€. "No problem. "Just come."" Closed for Lunch.

Le Passage   restaurant   French
10 rue Villars   tel. 04 42 37 09 00   www.le-passage.fr
Notes: €€. Reservations essential; request GF.

Restaurant Le Formal   restaurant   French
32 rue Espariat   tel. 04 42 27 08 31   www.restaurant-leformal.com
Notes: €€€. Must call in advance for GF.

La Coumpagnie   health food store   840 avenue Camp de Menthe

ANTIBES

Chez Helen   restaurant   International
35 rue des Revennes   tel. 04 92 93 88 52   www.chezhelen.fr/
Notes: €

La Forge   restaurant   French
10 rue Aubernon tel. 04 93 67 17 16   www.laforge-antibes.com
Notes: €€€€. Serve many celiacs. English spoken.

Le Figuier de Saint Esprit   restaurant   French
14 rue saint Esprit   tel. 04 93 34 50 12
www.restaurant-figuier-saint-esprit.com
Notes: €€€€. "Just come."

Gluten-Free F

ARLES

LA GRIGNOTTE   restaurant
6 rue Favorin   tel. 04 90 93 10 43   www.l
Notes: € - €€

Le Café des Mots   restaurant   bio/vergetarian
48 rue du Puits Neuf   tel. 04 42 21 67 52   www.lecafedesmots.fr
Notes: €

Le Cilantro   restaurant   international, Mediterranean
31 rue Porte de Laure   tel. 04 90 18 25 05   www.restaurantcilantro.com/
Notes: €€€

La Vie Claire   health food store   3 rue du Docteur Fanton

AUPS

L'Aiguiere   restaurant   French
Mar Joffre   tel. 04 94 70 12 40   www.laiguiere.fr
Notes: € - €€. "Yes, no problem. We have many celiac clients." Very nice staff.

AURIOL

Bio Estella   health food store   ZA Pont de Joux bât

AVIGNON

La Fourchette   restaurant   Bistro, French
17 rue Racine   tel. 04 90 85 20 93
Notes: €€€. Serve many celiacs, but no English spoken.

Maison Nani   restaurant   French
29 rue Theodore Aubaneil   tel. 04 90 14 07 30
Notes: €€

Biotope   health food store   5 rte de Lyon quartier St Lazare

BIOT

Cafe des Acacias   restaurant   French
5 rue St Sebastien   tel. 04 97 21 92 73
Notes: N/A. Advance notice necessary.

La Pierre a Four   restaurant   French
route de Valbonne   tel. 04 93 65 60 00
Notes: €€€. Advance notice necessary.

BONNIEUX

Arome   restaurant   French
ontemporary
2 rue Lucien Blanc   tel. 04 90 75 88 62   www.larome-restaurant.com/
Notes: €€ - €€€. Many celiac clients. English spoken.

Le Fournil   restaurant   French
5 place Carnot   tel. 04 90 75 83 62   www.lefournil-bonnieux.com
Notes: €€€€. Many celiac clients. English spoken.

Restaurant le Pont Julien   restaurant   French
D 900 | Quartier du Pont Julien   tel. 04 90 74 48 44 www.lepontjulien.com
Notes: € - €€. Many celiac clients. English spoken.

BRIGNOLES

Le Relais Bio   health food store
4 Chemin de Raton route Pré de Pâques RN7

CABRIES

Buffalo Grill   restaurant   French
Centre Cial Barneoud   tel. 04 42 02 54 73   www.buffalo-grill.fr
Notes: € - €€. This restaurant chain has a list of foods which are allergen-free
and gluten-free.

French Riviera (J. Friedman)

CANNES

Buffalo Grill   restaurant   French
rue du Professeur J. Rousselot 38 route de Douvres   tel. 02 31 95 50 40
www.buffalo-grill.fr
Notes: € - €€. This restaurant chain has a list of foods which are allergen-free
and gluten-free.

Chez Vincent et Nicolas   restaurant   Mediterranean
92 rue Meynadier   tel. 04 93 68 35 39
Notes: € - €€. Celiac clients. English spoken.

Ciro   restaurant   Italian
33 Bivouac Napoleon   tel. 04 93 39 21 24   www.cirocannes.com
Notes: N/A. Limited English spoken Italian spoken.

La Scena Lounge Bar & Restaurant restaurant   French
50 boulevard de la Croisette   tel. 04 92 99 70 00
http://www.marriott.com/hotels/hotel-information/restaurant/ncejw-palais-
stephanie/
Notes: €€€€. Will serve GF with advance notice. In Marriott Hotel.

Le Salon des Independants restaurant   Deli, French, Mediterranean
11 rue Louis Perrissol   tel. 04 93 39 97 06   le-salon-des-independants.fr
Notes: €€€. English spoken.

Restaurant 3.14   hotel/restaurant   International
5 rue François Einesy   tel. 04 92 99 72 09   www.3-14hotel.com
Notes: €€€€. GF dishes indicated on menu.

Palais Stephanie Marriott)   hotel with 2 restaurants   French
50 boulevard de la Croisette   tel. 04 92 99 70 00   www.marriott.com
Notes: €€€€

La Vie Claire   health food store   15 avenue du Général Vautrin

La Panorama Rooftop Bar   café/bar   French
50 boulevard de la Croisette   tel. 04 92 99 70 00   www.marriott.com
Notes: €€€€. Will serve GF with advance notice. In Palais Stephanie marriott
hotel.

CAP D'AIL

"Le Cap" Outdoor Terrace   restaurant
Port de Cap d'Ail   tel. 04 92 10 67 67   http://www.marriott.com
Notes: €€€€. Will serve GF with advance notice. In Riviera Marriott Hotel
La Porte de Monaco.

Riviera Marriott Hotel La Porte de Monaco   hotel with 2 restaurants
Port de Cap d'Ail   tel. 04 92 10 67 67   http://www.marriott.com
Notes: €€€€

Brasserie "Le Cap"   brasserie   brasserie
Port de Cap d'Ail   tel. 04 92 10 67 67   http://www.marriott.com
Notes: €€€€. Will serve GF with advance notice. In Riviera Marriott Hotel
La Porte de Monaco.

CAP D'ANTIBES

Restaurant De Bacon   restaurant   French
Bd. De Bacon   tel. 04 93 61 50 02   www.restaurantdebacon.com
Notes: €€€€. Advance notice necessary.

CARNOUX EN PROVENCE

Biocoop Carnoux   health food store   15 avenue Gay Lussac Z.I.

CARPENTRAS

C'Bio Traiteur   restaurant   bio
283 avenue Notre Dame de Santé   tel. 04 88 84 47 16   www.c-bio.net

La Vie Claire   health food store   375 av. Frédéric Mistral
Biocoop L'Auzonne   health food store   283 av. Notre Dame de Santé

CASSIS

La Defonce   restaurant   French
3 rue Laurent Ventron   tel. 04 42 01 28 33
Notes: N/A. Many celiac clients. English spoken.

LeBonaaparte   restaurant   Seafood, French
14 rue General Bonaparte   tel. 04 42 01 80 84
Notes: . Many celiac clients. English spoken.

CAVAILLON

Cultures Bio   health food store
Quartier Bel Air 1713 route de Robion

Sur le pont d'Avignon ... (J. Friedman)

CHATEAUNEUF-DU-PAPE

Hostellerie Chateau   restaurant   French
route de Sorgues   tel. 04 90 83 70 23   www.chateaufinesroches.com/
Notes: €€€€. Many celiac clients. English spoken.

La Maisouneta   restaurant   French
7 rue Joseph Ducros   tel. 04 90 32 55 03
Notes: € - €€. Many celiac clients. English spoken.

CHEMIN CAMBARNIER-NORD

Club Med Opio En Provence   all-inclusive resort   French
Chemin Cambarnier-Nord 06650   tel. 04 93 09 71 00
http://www.clubmed.com/cm/jsp/clubmed_welcome.jsp
Notes: €€€€

CORRENS

Auberge du Parc   restaurant   French
place Général de Gaulle   tel. 04 94 59 53 52   www.aubergeduparc.fr
Notes: €€€ - €€€€. Chef is very familiar with gluten-free issues.

COTIGNAC

Le Café du Cours   restaurant   brasserie
23 cours Gambetta   tel. 04 94 04 60 14
Notes: €. Will adapt many dishes to be GF.

DRAGUIGNAN

Au Fruit Defendu   restaurant   French
21 boulevard Liberte   tel. 04 94 68 85 66   http://www.lefruitdefendu.com/
Notes: €€€€

Lou Galoubet   restaurant   French
23 boulevard Jean Jaures   tel. 04 94 68 08 50   www.lougaloubet.fr
Notes: €€€. "Just come."

Soleil Bio   health food store
868 avenue Pierre Brossolette - ZA Pont de Lorgues

EYGALIERES

La Petite Table   restaurant   French
82 rue du Docteur Roque   tel. 04 90 38 19 23
Notes: €€€. Gluten-free on-demand with advance notice. English spoken.

EZE

La Taverne d'antan   restaurant/wine bar   wine bar
6 rue Plane   tel. 04 92 10 79 61   www.tavernedantan.com/
Notes: N/A. Celiac clients. English spoken.

Auberge du Cheval Blanc   restaurant   French
place de la Colette   tel. 04 93 41 03 17
http://www.aubergedelacroixdupape.com/
Notes: € - €€

FAYENCE

Le France   restaurant   French
1 Grande rue du Chateau   tel. 04 94 76 00 14
Notes: N/A. "Just come."

FONTAINE-DE-VAUCLUSE

Hostellerie le Chateau   restaurant   French
La Petite place   tel. 04 90 20 31 54
Notes: N/A. Many celiac clients. English spoken.

La Vanne Marel   restaurant   French
place Colonne   tel. 04 90 20 32 56
Notes: €€. Many celiac clients. English spoken.

Restaurant Petrarque   restaurant   French
place Colonne   tel. 04 90 20 31 48   www.petrarque-et-laure.com/
Notes: €€. Many celiac clients. English spoken.

Gluten-Free

Le Pa...
13 h...

Restaurant Philip   restaurant
Fontaine tel. 04 90 20 31 81
Notes: €€€. Many celiac clients. English spoken.

FREJUS
La Vie Claire   health food store   1592 ave de Lattre de Tass...

GOURDES
La Bastide de Gordes   restaurant   French
Le Village   tel. 04 90 72 12 12   www.bastide-de-gordes.com
Notes: €€€ - €€€€

Les Cuisines du Chateau   restaurant   French
place du Chateau   tel. 04 90 72 01 31
Notes: €€

GRASSE
La Bastide Saint Antoine-Jacques Chibois restaurant   French
48 avenue Henri dunant   tel. 04 93 70 94 94 www.jacques-chibois.com
Notes: €€€€. Reservations a must.

La Vie Claire   health food store   67 avenue de la Libération

ISLE SUR LA SORGUE
la Provete   restaurant   French
4 bis rue Jean-Jacques-Rousseau   tel. 04 90 38 57 29   www.la-prevote.fr
Notes: €€ - €€€

Le Mas de Cure-Bourse   restaurant   French
120 chemin de la Serre   tel. 04 90 38 16 58 www.masdecurebourse.com
Notes: € - €€

ISTRES
La table de Sébastien   restaurant   cuisine gastronomique
7 avenue Hélène Boucher   tel. 04 42 55 16 01 www.latabledesebastien.fr
Notes: €€€ - €€€€

Biocoop Provence   health food store   26 chemin des Bords de Crau
Biosphere   health food store   rue Monteaux- Les Baumes

JUAN-LES-PINS
L'Amiral   restaurant   French
7 avenue Amiral Courbet   tel. 04 93 67 34 61
Notes: €€€€

radis restaurant French
oulevard Edouard Baudoin | Residence Eden Beach   tel. 04 93 61 22 30
tp://www.restaurant-cote-d-azur.com
Notes: €€€€

LA MOTTE-D'AIGUES

Restaurant du Lac restaurant French
Etang de la Bonde   tel. 04 90 09 14 10   www.restaurantdulac.eu
Notes: €€€ - €€€€. Celiac clients. English spoken.

MANDELIEU LA NAPOULE

Restaurant Cote Place restaurant Mediterranean
21 place de la Fontaine   tel. 04 93 47 59 27
Notes: €. Serve many celiac customers. English spoken. Please call ahead.

MANDELIEU-LA NAPOULE

Le Boucanier restaurant seafood
Port de La Napoule   tel. 04 93 49 80 51   www.boucanier.fr
Notes: €€€. "Just come."

L'Oasis restaurant Provencal-Asian
rue J. H. Carle   tel. 04 93 49 95 52   www.oasis-raimbault.com
Notes: €€€. "Just come."

MARSEILLE

Au Bord De L'Eau restaurant Mediterranean
15 rue Des Arapedes | Port De La Madrague Montredon   tel. 04 91 72 68 04
http://www.auborddeleau.eu/
Notes: €€€. "Just come."

Buffalo Grill restaurant French
30 cours d'Estiennes d'Orves   tel. 04 91 59 83 78   www.buffalo-grill.fr
Notes: € - €€. This restaurant chain has a list of foods which are allergen-free
and gluten-free.

La cote de boeuf restaurant French
35 cours Honore d'Estienne d'Orves   tel. 04 91 33 00 25
www.marseille.com/la-cote-de-boeuf
Notes: €€€. "GF? Yes, of course!"

Lauracee restaurant French
96 rue Grignan   tel. 04 91 33 63 36   http://www.lelauracee.com/
Notes: €€€. Neighborhood: Saint-Victor. Advance notice necessary.

View outside Van Gogh's asylum window St Remy (J. Coyne)

Le Bistro Véntien   restaurant   French
29 cours Julien   tel. 04 91 47 34 34
Notes: N/A

Le Petit Nice   restaurant   French
Anse de Maldorme   tel. 04 91 59 25 92   http://www.petitnice-passedat.com/
Notes: €€€€. English spoken. "Just come."

Bio Coin Joli	health food store	14 boulevard Ganay
Biocoop Castellane	health food store	87 rue d'Italie
Biocoop Des Collines	health food store	203 route des Camoins
La Vie Claire	health food store	14 blvd Georges Clémenceau

MARTIGUES
Le Garage   restaurant   cuisine gastronomique
20 avenue Frederic Mistral   tel. 04 42 44 09 51
www.restaurantmartigues.com
Notes: Staff very familiar with gluten-free.

MENERBES

Le Galoubet   restaurant   French
104 avenue Marcellin Poncet   tel. 04 90 72 36 08
Notes: N/A. "Of course. Just come!"

Hostellerie Le Roy Soleil   inn, restaurant   French
Rte. Des Beaumettes   tel. 04 90 72 25 61   www.roy-soleil.com
Notes: €€€. Advance notice nessicary. GF breakfast.

MENTON

A Braijade Meridiounale   restaurant   French
66 rue Longue   tel. 04 93 35 65 65
Notes: N/A

La Coquile d'Or   restaurant   French
1 quai Bonaparte   tel. 04 93 35 80 67
Notes: N/A. "Yes, of course, just come!"

Port Garavan   restaurant   Italian
Nouveau Port de Menton Garavan   tel. 04 93 28 85 56
www.restaurantgaravan.com
Notes: €€ - €€€. "Just come."

Restaurant Le Galion   restaurant   French
Nouveau Port de Menton Garavan   tel. 04 93 35 89 73
Notes: N/A. "Just come."

MONTE-CARLO (IN MONACO)

La Maison du Caviar   restaurant   French
1 avenue Saint-Charles   tel. 377 93 30 80 06
Notes: €€€€. "Just come."

Le Cafe de Paris   restaurant   brasserie
place du Casino   tel. 377 98067676
Notes: €€€€. Reservations and advance notice for GF necessary.

Le Grill   restaurant   grill
place du Casino | Hôtel de Paris   tel. 377 98 06 88 88
en.hoteldeparismontecarlo.com/Le-Grill,252.html
Notes: €€€€. Reservations recommended. Let them know then that you need a GF meal.

Le Louis XV - Alain Ducasse   restaurant   Mediterranean
place du Casino   tel. 377 92162976   www.alain-ducasse.com
Notes: €€€€. Reservations and advance notice for GF necessary.

Pulcinella   restaurant   Italian
17 rue du Portier   tel. 377 93 30 73 61   www.pulcinella.mc
Notes: €€€€. "Just come." English spoken.

Zelo's   restaurant   Mediterranean
10 Ave Princesse Grace | Grimaldi Forum   tel. 37799992550
Notes: €€€€. "Just come."

MOUGINS
La Place de Mougins   restaurant   French
41 place du Commandant Lamy   tel. 04 93 90 15 78
http://www.laplacedemougins.com/presentation.html
Notes: €€€€. Yes, of course! Advance notice necessary.

Le Bistrot de Mougins   restaurant   Provencal
Pl. du Village   tel. 04 93 75 78 34
Notes: €€. Many celiac clients. "Just come."

Le Rendez Vous de Mougins   restaurant   French
84 place Commandant Lamy   tel. 04 93 75 87 47
Notes: €€. Reservations necessary.

La Vie Claire   health food store   118 chemin de Carimaï

NICE
Argane Bio   restaurant   bio/vegetarian
35 avenue Maréchal Foch   tel. 04 93 62 86 12   bioos.c.la
Notes: €. Many GF dishes.

Au Moulin Enchante   restaurant   French
rue Barberis   tel. 04 93 55 33 14   www.aumoulinenchante.com
Notes: €€

Bioos   restaurant   Bio
12 rue Alberti   tel. 04 93 01 94 70

Boni   restaurant   Italian
15 rue Tonduti de l'Escarene   tel. 04 93 62 93 36
boniresto.monsite.orange.fr/
Notes: €€. Celiac clients. English spoken.

Havelie   restaurant   Indian
35 rue d'angleterre   tel. 04 93 88 99 40   www.restaurant-havelie.com
Notes: €€€ - €€€€. Neighborhood: Notre-Dame

Keisuke Matsushima   restaurant   French
2 2 rue de la France Vieux Nice   tel. 04 93 82 26 06
www.keisukematsushima.com
Notes: €€€€. Reservations essential. Indicate GF then.

Le Chantecler   restaurant   French
37 promenade des Anglais   tel. 04 93 16 64 00
http://www.hotel-negresco-nice.com/en/restaurant-bars/chantecler
Notes: €€€€. Celiac clients. English spoken.

Le Dauphin Nicois   restaurant   Mediterranean
31 bld de la madeleine   tel. 04 93 97 02 22
http://www.dauphinnicois.com/restaurant-nice
Notes: € - €€. "Yes, absolutely!" Advance notice necessary.

Luc Salsedo   restaurant   French
14 rue Maccarani   tel. 04 93 82 24 12
http://www.restaurant-salsedo.com
Notes: €€€. Neighborhood: Liberti - Albert 1er

Menton with Roquebrunne and Monte Carlo (J. Coyne)

Biocoop Azur	health food store	59 bd Delfino
Biocoop Riviera	health food store	104 avenue Henri Dunant
La Vie Claire	health food store	Espace Nikaia 2 rue Dr Robini
La Vie Claire Nice Lamartine	health food store	18 rue Lamartine

NIMES

Au Flan Coco   restaurant   French
21 rue du Grand Couvent   tel. 04 66 21 84 81
Notes: €€ - €€€

La Table d'Auguste   restaurant   French
3 rue Nationale   tel. 04 66 67 74 57
Notes: € - €€. Call in the afternoon for GF for dinner.

Le Bistrot Nimois   restaurant   French
22 rue de la Curaterie   tel. 04 66 36 15 75   www.lebistrotnimois.com/
Notes: € - €€

Les Magnolias   restaurant   French
place Esclafidous   tel. 04 66 21 64 01
Notes: N/A

OLLIOULES

Restaurant Bio La Terrasse   restaurant   bio/vegetarian
1256 avenue Jean Monnet Espace Piedardan bâtiment 7
tel. 04 94 25 78 08   www.le-restaurant-bio.com
Notes: €€. GF, DF, vegetarian dishes.

PEIPIN - SISTERONTEL

La Vie Claire   health food store   Impasse de la Feniere

ROUSSILLON

Mas de Garrigon   restaurant   French
Rte.de St-Saturn-d' Apt   tel. 04 90 05 63 22
www.masdegarrigon-provence.com
Notes: €€€

SAINT MAXIMIN

La Vie Claire   health food store   ZAC du Chemin d"Aix

SAINT MITRE LES REMPARTS

Biocoop Des Cigales   health food store rue Saladelles ZAC des Etangs

SAINT REMY DE PROVENCE

La Gousse d'Ail   restaurant   Mediterranean
6 boulevard Marceau   tel. 04 90 92 16 87   www.la-goussedail.com/
Notes: €€€ - €€€€. Yes of course! Advance reservations necessary.

Le Bistrot Decouverte   restaurant   Mediterranean
19 bld Victor Hugo   tel. 04 90 92 34 49   www.bistrotdecouverte.com/
Notes: €€ - €€€€. Advance notice necessary.

Le Bistrot Nimois   restaurant   Mediterranean
22 rue de la Curaterie   tel. 04 66 36 15 75   www.lebistrotnimois.com
Notes: €

L'Olivade   restaurant   Provencal
12 rue du Chateau   tel. 04 90 92 52 74
Notes: €€. Advance notice necessary.

Restaurant Gastronomique de l'Hotel du Vallon de Valrugues
restaurant   Mediterranean
Chemin de Canto Cigalo   tel. 04 90 92 04 40
www.restaurant-marcdepassorio.com
Notes: €€€ - €€€€. Please call 2 days ahead for GF.

ST PAUL DE VENCE

La Colombe d'Or   inn, restaurant   French
Pl. General-de-Gaulle   tel. 04 93 32 80 02   www.la-colombe-dor.com
Notes: €€€€. Advance notice nessicary.

Hostellerie les Remparts   hotel, restaurant   French
72 rue Grande   tel. 04 93 32 09 88
Notes: €. Advance notice nessicary.

ST TROPEZ

Auberge des Maures   restaurant   French
4 rue Doct Bouttin   tel. 04 94 97 01 50   www.aubergedesmaures.fr/
Notes: €€€€. "Just come." Many dishes are GF.

L'Escale   restaurant   French
9 Quai Jean Joures   tel. 04 94 97 00 63
www.joseph-saint-tropez.com/lescale/index.html
Notes: N/A. "Just come."

ST-JEAN-CAP-FERRAT

Le Sloop   restaurant   French
Port de Plaisance   tel. 04 93 01 48 63
Notes: €€€

ST-RAPHAEL

L'Arbousier   restaurant   French
6 av. Valescure   tel. 04 94 95 25 00   www.arbousier.net
Notes: N/A. "But of course!" Advance notice necessary.

TOULON

Le Pointilliste   restaurant   seafood
43 rue Picot in Haute Ville   tel. 04 94 71 06 01
www.lepointilliste.com/?Accueil
Notes: €€€

Les Têtes d'Ail   restaurant   Provencal
22 rue des Cupboards   tel. 04 94 62 07 64
Notes: €. Will adapt dishes to be GF. Advance notice preferable.

La Vie Claire   health food store   39 rue Paul Landrin

VAISON LA ROMAINE

Nature Élements   health food store
2 avenue Alexandre Blanc - place de la Cathédrale

VENCE

Larmoise   restaurant   French
9 place Peyra   tel. 04 93 58 19 29   www.larmoise.com/
Notes: €€€. Celiac clients. English spoken.

VILLEFRANCHE SUR MER

La Mayssa   restaurant   French
Pl. Wilson   tel. 04 93 01 75 08   www.lemayssa.fr
Notes: €€ - €€€. Many plates are already gluten-free.

VILLENEUVE-LÈS-AVIGNON

Les Jardins d'été de la Chartreuse restaurant   organic/bio
58 rue de la République La Chartreuse   tel. 04 90 15 24 23
www.chartreuse.org/28/7/le-restaurant-de...
Notes: €

YSSINGEAUX

Biocoop Des Sucs Za   health food store La Guilde – Chatimbarbe

C'Bio Traiteur   restaurant   bio
262 avenue de l'Europe   tel. 04 90 63 31 07   www.c-bio.net

Biocoop Pre Vert 2   health food store
22 avenue de la Capelette

Menton Looking Down at Cap Martin (J. Coyne)

THE MIDI-PYRÉNÉES

Farmers Market Goose Eggs (R. Levy)

Chambres d'hôtes et gîte sans gluten

Marie-Laure Tauzin
Village
31230 Montbernard
tel. 05 61 94 19 60
http://www.chambresdhotes-sansgluten.fr/
delbosc-tauzin@wanadoo.fr

Marie-Laure and Alain welcome you to their "gluten free B&B", la Montbernardine, built in 1809, situated in a very small village, Montbernard. **They specialize in providing gluten free meals** suitable for celiac diets for family reasons: their daughter has celiac disease and other family members have gluten intolerance. Their meals are always gluten-free to avoid problems. You can rest assured that eating gluten free can be good fun ...

Breakfasts are continental. Here, you will be immersed in french culture, experiencing the language, cooking and customs.
Near the B&B:

L'isle en Dodon	10km	Aurignac	15km
Boulogne sur Gesse	12km	Saint Gaudens	34km
Ciadoux	6km	Montmaurin	15km

Muriska Bed and Breakfast

Maison Muriska
11 rue Dongaitz Anaiak
64122Urrugne
contact: Christine & Hervé
Labescau
tel: 06 89 43 85 26
www.muriska.com

A contemporary villa in the heart of Urrugne, a beautiful Basque village in South West France near the Atlantic Ocean with views of the Pyrénées mountains. The villa is also near the famous town of St Jean de Luz. All are 10 minutes by car. The Spanish border is 7km away and offers other exciting places to explore, including, San Sebastian, Bilbao and Guernica.

Christine and Hervé prepare a delicious breakfast each morning for guests and can easily make it **gluten-free** upon request. Muriska is non-smoking and animals are not allowed.

Bright and comfortable, the delightful bedroom for two people has direct access to the garden where you can take tea, read or prepare for your next day. The bedroom has a private shower and toilet. The library offers you a choice of books on the Basque culture and region, its history and gastronomy.

Prices are based on overnight stay for 2 persons (breakfast and tourist tax included). For single occupancy, deduct 5 €.
- January, February, March, April, 55 €
- May, June, July, August, September, 60 €
- October, November, December, 55 €
Arrivals between 5pm and 7pm. Departures by 11am.

ALBI

Ambroisie   restaurant   French
4 rue Henri Toulouse Lautrec   tel. 05 63 76 43 56
Notes:They have many celiac clients and can make many dishes gluten-free.
Extremely nice staff.
Notes: €€

Le Clos Sainte Cecile   restaurant   French
3 rue du Castelviel   tel. 05 63 38 19 74
Notes: Many choices for celiacs and many celiac clients. Reservations a
must.
Notes: €€

Le Jardin des Quatre Saisons   restaurant   French
19 boulevard de Strasbourg   tel. 05 63 60 77 76
www.lejardindesquatresaisons.fr/
Notes: €€

Restaurant Le Parvis   restaurant   French
27 place Sainte-Cecile   tel. 05 63 46 27 10 www.restaurantleparvis.com
Notes: €€ - €€€

AUCH
Les Jardins D'Augusta health food store   52 rue du 8 mai 1945

CAHORS
Biocoop Cahors   health food store   Chemin de Belle Croix
La Vie Claire   health food store   11 rue St. James

CASTELNAU DE MONTMIRAL
Le Dôme de Montmiral   restaurant   bio/vegetarian
Côte Rouge   tel. 05 63 57 26 78   www.domedemontmiral.com
Notes: €€. Restaurant only open by reservation.

CASTRES
Biocoop La Chartreuse health food store   2 rue Henri le Chatelier

CONDOM
Arc En Ciel   health food store   22 rue de la République

FENOUILLET
Biocoop L'Oustal   health food store   22 rue de la cité Saint Gobain

GERM EN LOURON

Auberge de Germ hotel French
tel. 05 62 99 90 86 http://www.auberge-de-germ.com/
Notes: €€

LABEGE

Biocoop Grandeur Nature Labege health food store
Z.A.C. de la Bourgade - route de Baziège - Lieudit "Lameras"

LANDORTHE

Bio Comminges health food store
Zone commerciale de Landorthe – RN 117

LOURDES

La Solitude restaurant French
3 passe Saint-Louis / Ave B. Soubirous tel. N/A book via 3rd party
Notes: N/A

MILLAU

Biocoop Du Cres health food store
465 boulevard Georges Brassens

MONTBERNARD

Chambres d'hôtes et Gîte Sans Gluten Marie-Laurie Tauzin
hotel rooms, B&B tel. 05 61 94 19 60 http://chambresdhotes-sansgluten.fr

Amaranthe health food store 26 rue A. Einstein

MURET

Biocoop Muret health food store 20 boulevard Joffrery

ODOS

Biocoop Tarbes health food store 77 route de Lourdes

ONET LE CHÂTEAU

Biocoop Campana health food store 76 bis route de Séverac

PERPIGNAN

La Crêperie du Théâtre restaurant creperie
12 rue du Théâtre tel. 04 68 34 29 06 www.creperie-du-theatre.fr
Notes: €. Can get delicious GF crepes.

Le Bacchus   restaurant   French
9 avenue Julien Panchot   tel. 04 68 54 16 86   www.le-bacchus.fr/
Notes: €€

Le Grain de Folie   restaurant   French
71 avenue Gen Leclerc   tel. 04 68 51 00 50
legraindefolieperpignan@orange.fr
Notes: €. Many celiac clients. Advance notice.

Hotel Restaurant La Fauceille   hotel, restaurant   French
860 Chemin de la Fauceille   tel. 04 68 21 09 10   www.lafauceille.com/
Notes: €€€€. Advance notice necessary.

PRADES
El Patio   restaurant   French
19 place de la Republique   tel. 04 68 05 35 60
Notes: €

PY
La Fontaine   restaurant/hotel   French
24 Carrer Major   tel. 04 68 96 50 79   restaurantdepy.ifrance.com
Notes: € - €€. Chef is gluten-intolerant and will make many GF dishes and breakfast.

QUINT FONSEGRIVES
Biocoop Natur'Eol   health food store   12 chemin de Ribaute

RABASTENS
L'Epi Se Rit   health food store   13 place Guillaume du Cunh

SAINT AFFRIQUE
Lou Cussou   health food store   101 avenue Jean Jaurès

SAINT ANTONIN NOBLE VAL
3 Cantons   Camping   French
Saint Antonin Noble Val   tel. 05 63 31 98 57   www.3cantons.eu
Notes: €

SAINT CERE
Coloquinte   health food store   1 boulevard Gambetta

SAINT MENOUX
L'Echoppe   health food store   Domaine de la Mhotte

TARBES

Biocoop Tarbes Ouest   health food store   rue de la Garounère

TOULOUSE

Anges et Demons   restaurant   French
1 rue Perchepinte   tel. 05 61 52 66 69
www.restaurant-angesetdemons.com/
Notes: €€€€

Au Pois Gourmand   restaurant   French
3 rue Emile Heybrard   tel. 05 34 36 42 00   http://www.pois-gourmand.fr/
Notes: €€€€. Reservations are a must.

Chez Emile   restaurant   French
13 pl St Georges   tel. 05 61 21 05 56   www.restaurant-emile.com/
Notes: €€€€

Le Genty Magre   restaurant   French
3 rue Genty Magre   tel. 05 61 21 38 60   www.legentymagre.com
Notes: €€€ - €€€€. They can make many dishes that are gluten-free. Very
nice staff.

Le Varsi Café   restaurant   French
1 rue Marthe Varsi   tel. 05 61 42 00 88
Notes: €€€

Manger Autrement   restaurant   Bio/vegetarian
155 Grande rue St Michel   tel. 05 61 32 68 41 www.resto-bio-toulouse.com
Notes: €. Plenty of GF dishes.

Saveurs Bio   restaurant   Bio/vegetarian
22 rue Maurice Fonvielle   tel. 05 61 12 15 15   saveursbio.com
Notes: €. Plenty of GF dishes.

Van Gogh   restaurant   French
21 place St Gerges Wilson neighborhood   tel. 05 61 21 03 15
http://www.vangoghtoulouse.fr/
Notes: €€€ - €€€€

Biocoop Purpan health food store   301 avenue de Grande Bretagne
Grandeur Nature health food store   21 av. des Ecoles Jules Julien

TOULOUSE ROQUE SUR GARONNE

Buffalo Grill   restaurant   French
40 avenue des Eglantines   tel. 05 61 76 95 10   www.buffalo-grill.fr
Notes: € - €€. This restaurant chain has a list of foods which areallergen free and gluten-free.

TOURNEFEUILLE

Biocoop La Ramee   health food store   110 avenue du Marquisat

URRUGNE

Muriska Bed And Breakfast B&B   French
11 rue Dongaitz Anaiak   tel. 06 89 43 85 26   www.muriska.com
Notes: €€ - €€€. Specializes in gluten-free.

VERNET

Le Cortal   restaurant   French
Chateau   tel. 04 68 05 55 79
http://bistrot-lecortal.fr/default.aspx
Notes: €. No need to call for GF. Just come in.

LANGUEDOC-ROUSSILLON

Une scene jolie (J. Friedman)

Chambres d'hôtes à Carcassonne
Brigitte and Robert Calmon
Domaine Saint Louis Maquens
11090 Carcassonne, Aude
Languedoc Roussillon
tel. 04 68 47 52 46,   06 13 18 14 04
brigitte.calmon @ free.fr
http://chambresdhotes-sansgluten.fr

Located just outside the town of Carcassonne, in the hamlet of Maquens, near the airport, golf, Lake Cavayère., in the center of the Aude department, and in the midst of historic sites. There are many sites to visit: the city of Carcassonne, the Cathar castles, Canal du Midi, abbeys, the chasm Cabrespine Limousis caves, the papermill and Brousses Villaret , Rennes le Chateau and its enigmatic Abbé Saunière, Golf 2 km, swimming (45 min or Mediterranean lake 10 min), Limoux carnival, etc. For wine lovers, it is possible to visit the cellars to be alone with your car, or visit organized by small groups. The region is rich in different wines and the many restaurants serve the famous cassoulet de Carcassonne.

The property has for rent 4 cottages with private bathrooms, including 2 very large family rooms. Brigitte prepares gourmet breakfasts of homemade cakes, croissants, pastries and bread or buns, homemade jams, cheese, sausage and cereal, coffee, tea or chocolate. **With advance notice, Brigitte will make you a cake or cookies without gluten.**

AIGUES-MORTES

Biocoop Fleur De Sel Zac health food store   Terre de Camargue

ALES

Soleil Levain   health food store   16 avenue Jules Guesde

BAGNOLS SUR CEZE

Biocoop Mere Nature health food store   route de Saint Gervais

BALARUC-LE-VIEUX

Biocoop De L'Étang De Thau health food store
Chemin de Colombet – ZAE La Barrière

BEZIERS

La Vie Claire   health food store   31 rue de la Citadelle

BOURG EN BRESSE

Mag'Bio   health food store   10 boulevard Kennedy

CANET-EN-ROUSSILLON

Biocoop Canet-En-Roussillon health food store   1 rue Paul Emile Victor

CARCASSONNE

Tourne Sol   health food store   Allée Gutenberg /ZI La Bourriette

Chambres D'hôtes À Carcassonne B&B   French
Domaine Saint Louis Maquens   tel. 04 68 47 52 46
Notes: €€€. Specializes in gluten-free.

Le Parc Franck Putelat   restaurant   French
Chemin des Anglais   tel. 04 68 71 80 80
http://www.restaurantleparcfranckputelat.fr/
Notes: €€€ - €€€€

Restaurant Chez Fred   restaurant and take-away   French
31 bd Omer-Sarrault -   tel. 04 68 72 02 23   www.chez-fred.fr
Notes: €€€. GF menu

Restaurant La Marquie   restaurant   French
13 rue St Jean   tel. 04 68 71 52 00   www.lamarquiere.com
Notes: €€

CÉRET

La Fontaine   restaurant   French
place des Neuf Jets   tel. 04 68 87 23 47
Notes: €€

CLAIRA
Biocoop Cosmos Claira health food store   route du Barcarès

COLLIOURE
Casa Leon   restaurant   French
2 rue Riere   tel. 04 68 82 10 74
Notes: €

L'Amphitrion   restaurant   seafood
17 rue Jean Bart   tel. 04 68 82 36 00
Notes: N/A

Le Dali   restaurant   French
21 place Jean Jaures   tel. 04 68 83 93 01
Notes: N/A

CRUZY
L'Auberge de la Croisade restaurant   French
Hameau de la Croisade   tel. 04 67 89 36 36
http://www.auberge-de-la-croisade.com/
Notes: €€ - €€€€. Will adapt dishes to be GF.

LE CRES / MONTPELLIER
Germe De Vie   health food store   10 route de Nimes

LIMOUX
Floreal   health food store   41 avenue Fabre d'Eglantine

MENDE
La Claire Fontaine   health food store   Impasse Four Moulon

MONTPELLIER
Atys Café   restaurant   bio/vegetarian
5 place de la Révolution Française   tel. 04 67 85 01 98   www.atyscafe.fr
Notes: €. GF dishes readily available.

Cabiron Boutique   boutique   French
Odysseum   tel. 04 99 64 58 54
Notes: €. Ice cream, artisanal chocolates and macaroons, all gluten-free

Des Lys   restaurant   Bio/vegetarian
39 place du Millénaire antigone   tel. 04 99 64 42 03
Notes: €. Dine in and take out. Restaurant is only open for lunch.

La Reserve Rimbaud   restaurant   French
820 avenue St Maur   tel. 04 67 72 52 53   www.reserve-rimbaud.com/
Notes: €€€€

Le Jardin des Sens   hotel/restaurant   French
11 avenue St Lazarre   tel. 04 99 58 38 38
www.jardindessens.com/index.html
Notes: €€€€

Le Méridien   restaurant/café   bio/vegetarian
rue Elie Wiesel Bassin Jacque Coeur Port Marianne   tel. 04 67 20 97 54
www.meridien34.fr
Notes: €€ - €€€. Can make GF dishes easily.

Leon de Bruxelles   restaurant   Belgian
108 AV Pirée Esplanade de l'Europe   tel. 02 41 72 38 38
www.leon-de-bruxelles.fr
Notes: €€€. This restaurant is part of a large chain all over France. They have
limited items that are GF, but their Director of Quality Control nationwide
provided us with a list of menu items that are GF. See page 16.

Los Caracolès   restaurant   Spanish
8 place Alexandre Laissac   tel. 04 99 06 04 94 www.bodegaloscaracoles.fr/
Notes: €€. Owners very familiar with GF and will make GF tapas.

O'coing   restaurant   Traditional
2 place de Strasbourg   tel. 04 67 64 01 88   www.o-coing.com
Notes: €€

NARBONNE

Ave Domitius   restaurant   French
16 Hotel de Ville   tel. 04 68 32 33 76
Notes: N/A. Reservations are a must, at least a week ahead.

Buffalo Grill   restaurant   French
Croix Sud route de Perpignan   tel. 04 68 41 43 72   www.buffalo-grill.fr
Notes: € - €€. This restaurant chain has a list of foods which areallergen free
and gluten-free.

La Table du Chateau   restaurant   French
16 rue de Paris | Bizanet   tel. 04 68 93 51 19
latableduchateau.fr/en/contact.php
Notes: €€ - €€€€

Restaurant L'Estagnol   restaurant   French
12 avenue Narbonne   tel. 04 68 49 01 27   http://lestagnol.fr/
Notes: €€

La Vie Claire   health food store   2 route de Gruissan - Espace Soleil
Biocoop Terrabio   health food store   36-A bd Marcel Sembat

PERPIGNAN
Cosmos   health food store   12 avenue de Prades
La Vie Claire   health food store   948 Chemin de La Fauceille

PRADES
La Plantula   health food store   7 rue de la Basse

REMOULINS
La Crêpe Rit   restaurant   creperie
2 place des Grands Jours   tel. 04 66 57 24 93   www.la-crepe-rit.fr
Notes: €

SAINT HIPPOLYTE DU FORT
La Fourmi Et La Cigale   health food store   16 boulevard des Remparts

SAINTE ENIMIE
La Jasse   B&B   French
rue de la Combe   tel. 04 66 48 53 96
http://www.barbierlajasse.fr/la_demeure.html
Notes: €€€

SAINT-MARTIN-DE-LONDRES
Les Muscardins   restaurant   Cuisine gastronomique
19 route des Cévennes   tel. 04 67 55 75 90   www.les-muscardins.fr
Notes: €€€€. GF dishes available.

UZES
La Marigoule 2   health food store   30 bld Jean Jaurès
YZEURE
L'Esperluette   health food store   43 ter rue des Epoux Contoux

SAMPLE "GLUTEN-FREE-ADAPTABLE" MENU FOR CHEZ FRED

The chef is willing to adapt most menu items on the regular menu to be gluten-free for his many celiac clients. He indicates which choices can be adapted to be gluten-free with the words *solution coeliaque possible*. He changes the menu regularly but, for the purposes of this book, has offered this sample menu (which we then translated into English) of gluten-free items. *Merci beaucoup*, Chef Fred!

Bistro Menu · (served regularly except weekends and holidays)

Starter + main dish OR starter + dessert €15.00 lunch / €18.00 dinner
Starter + main dish + dessert or espresso €18.00 lunch / €22.00 dinner
Bistro Dish (lunch only) €10.00

Caesar Salad of country guinea fowl and quail eggs a la plancha (no croutons)   OR Suggestion of the day ·

Wok beef with vegetables, penne rigate and fresh coriander (without the penne) OR Dish of the day

Dessert of the day OR Café Espresso

Menu Gourmand Carcassonnais € 26.00

Tangy honey on arugula and corn salad, foie gras mi-cuit and gizzards OR skewered shrimp a la plancha, with raw "Thai" vegetables and Suquet Sea saffron
OR pear beef, butter and two mustards and homemade fries (no sauce)

Apple crumble ® Marseillette walnut crumble (can make GF)
Ripened cheeses

Menu Carcassonnais Gastronome € 30.00

Pumpkin tiramisu, foie gras with gingerbread (GF with no bread or tiramisu)
OR Sea bream fillet smoked by us at our chestnut woods and mountains The Martys "Croustet" Tapenade with Olives ® Fabi (GF without Croustet)

Jacques-roasted scallops with truffle-infused jus and mushroom risotto OR Cassoulet or house sausage and country pork, duck confit and beans Castelnaudary ®

Ripened cheeses

The Menu Mômes For children - 8 years, accompanied by their parents taking a meal € 10.00

Grilled Fish and salad or skewers of beef, home fries, green salad
ice cream OR sweet banana and mint "liquorice" (and fun toy!)

Please note that this menu is subject to change frequently. If you have an allergy to gluten, peanuts, or something else, please tell me before ordering. Thank you.

AQUITAINE

Les Fleurs pour Annalise (R. Levy)

Château de Villars
Chateau de Villars
Pres de la cure
24530 Villars
tel. 0 5 53 03 41 58
www.chateaude villars.com/fr

'Chateau de Villars offers weeklong and 10 day Full Board 'Gluten Free' holidays in a friendly & casual environment with 9 acres of tranquillity & beauty in the heart of the Dordogne, South West France. **The kitchen is always gluten-free so there is no concern of cross contamination. Those with other special dietary concerns are also welcome.**

Enjoy the idyllic countryside, the quaint villages, the quietness, the fresh air, the clear night skies & the Chateau's relaxed lifestyle in 10 day and weeklong "Relax & Learn" activity holidays. The group is small; with a maximum of 12 guests at any one time. During and included in the price of each "Relax & Learn" activity holiday, there are three outings and the 3 "marvels" of Villars are all in walking/biking distance – Chateau de Puyguilem, Abbaye de Boschaud and the Grottes de Villars!

All rooms have private bath or shower, with the option of different bed configurations (King, Queen, Double, Single) – three rooms can be configured for separate beds (two single beds or two double beds). Access to pool and Chateau Spa room for Beauty treatment (manicure, pedicure, facial), reflexology and massage.

Included are the following:
- 6 full days and 7 nights
- Continental Breakfast each morning during your week.
- Light lunches at the Chateau or picnic provided each day.
- 4 course dinners each night with two glasses of Bergerac wine.

For your "Relax & Learn" Activity you can choose from:

- Paint & Sketching
- Market Tours & Cooking
- Walking, Strolling & Photography
- "Bergerac Wineries"
- "'Ooooh La La' –Fun with French Language & Culture"
- OR

"The Chateau de Villars 'Hands On' Gluten Free Cooking Week"
Mouth-watering! September 25 – October 2, 2011

Finally what you've all been waiting for – and asking for – a chance to cook with Bill Davies and Richard Wells – and to experience the unique location of the new teaching kitchen at 'La Maison' – an 18th century house adjoining the Chateau. The day begins with an outing to one of our local French markets. We will stroll among the stalls, selecting the best seasonal ingredients for our feast! Afterwards, we'll relax at a cafe, talk about cooking and watch the French world go by. Then we'll head back to 'La Maison'. Starting the preparation, we'll review our menu and recipes in detail and then begin chopping, cutting, dicing, laughing, baking, tasting…and, of course, all with a glass of local wine in hand. Afterwards, we'll all sit down together - joined by the other Chateau guests who are not cooking – to enjoy and experience the fruits of our labour, with pairings of Bergerac wines.

You will also have the chance to join sessions for baking, pastry making and hors d'oeuvres during the week. On the first day, you'll be given your own Chateau apron (yours to take away when you leave) and, during the week, print outs of all of the recipes used.

La Belle Demeure B&B

Lieu-dit Le Bouscot,
24250 St. Cybranet, France
www.labelledemeure.com
E-Mail: frogetrosbif@wanadoo.fr
Tel. 05 53 28 57 12

Ideally situated in the Périgord Noir, La Belle Demeure is the perfect place to take that relaxing and well-deserved break. Just 9 miles from the medieval town of Sarlat and 2 miles from the Dordogne Valley, La Belle Demeure is nestled in the Céou Valley, halfway along the road between the Bastide town of Domme and the striking castle of Castelnaud. There are many of the most visited sites in the region very nearby such as Sarlat, Beynac, La Roque Gageac, Josephine Baker's Chateau Les Milandes, Lascaux II etc ..., so there is always somewhere new to explore in this pretty corner of the Dordogne and you will never be short of something to do. What with over 250 miles of way-marked walking trails and cycling tracks

You can take the option of a delicious evening meal served 'Table d'Hôtes' style whether it be in the dining room, or outside on the terrace shaded by its century-old vine over-looking the swimming pool. Home cooked dishes like Duck Confit with Pommes Sarladaises (with garlic and parsley), Périgordine Lasagne, Gratin de Confit de canard aux marrons (a duck and potato dish with chestnuts), Whiskey flamed chicken en croute, terrine with onion marmalade, local goat's cheese and spinach tart and many others. For desert, try the walnut cake, an apple clafoutis, homemade 'parfait' ice-cream or Bread and Butter Pudding à la Brioche.

Dinner is 22 Euros per person (without drinks) and to accompany your meal you can choose one of our personally selected Bergerac wines, or from a selection of non-alcoholic drinks.

Evening meals are served most nights of the week, but not all. If you are interested in having dinner on the night you arrive, do request in advance and/or check to see if dinner will be served that particular night.

Please make it clear in advance if you are vegetarian or gluten-free or have any major food allergies or dislikes, as most things can be adapted with advance notice.

AGEN

Au Pre Vert   health food store   156 impasse Péchabout

AINHOA

Hotel Ithurria   hotel, restaurant   French
place du Fronton   tel. 05 59 29 92 11   hotel@ithurria.com
Notes: €€€

ANGLET

Bio Parme   health food store   Z.A de Parme RN 10

ARTIGUES PRES BORDEAUX

Biocoop Artigues   health food store   25 avenue de l'Ile de Italie

BAYONNE

Auberge Du Cheval Blanc   restaurant   French
68 rue Bourgneuf   tel. 05 59 59 01 33
Notes: €€€€. Please note that this is not an in; it is just a restaurant. Advance
notice necessary

Bayonnais   restaurant   French
38 quai Corsaires   tel. 05 59 25 61 19
Notes: €€€ - €€€€. Advance notice necessary.

La Feuillantine   restaurant   French
21 Quai Amiral Dubourdieu   tel. 05 59 46 14 94
http://www.lafeuillantine-bayonne.com/
Notes: €€€ - €€€€. "No problem."

La Grange   restaurant   French
28 Quai Galuperie   tel. 05 59 46 17 84
Notes: €€ - €€€. "No problem."

Restaurant El Asador   restaurant   French
19 rue Vieille Boucherie   tel. 05 59 59 08 57
Notes: €€ - €€€. Advance notice necessary.

Restaurant Miura   restaurant   Basque
24 rue Marengo   tel. 05 59 59 49 89
Notes: €€ - €€€

Bio Etika   health food store   7 avenue du Maréchal Juin
La Vie Claire   health food store   14 rue Pilori

BERGERAC

L'Imparfait   restaurant   French
8 rue Fontaines   tel. 05 53 57 47 92
Notes: €€. Many celiac clients. Request GF in advance.

Biocoop Bergerac Sud   health food store   71 avenue Paul Doumer
La Vie Claire   health food store   65 rue du Docteur Roux

BEYNAC ET CAZENAC

La Petite Tonelle   restaurant   Local French
Le Bourg   tel. 05 53 29 95 18
Notes: €€ - €€€

BIARRITZ

Chez Pilou   restaurant/bistro   Bistro
3 rue Larralde   tel. 05 59 24 11 73
Notes: €€€. "Yes of course."

Chez Ospi   restaurant   French
6 rue Jean Bart   tel. 05 59 24 64 98   http://www.chezospi.com/
Notes: €€

Il Giardino   restaurant   Italian
62 rue Gambetta   tel. 05 59 22 16 41   ilgiardino-biarritz.com
Notes: €

La Table d'Aranda   restaurant   French
87 avenue de la Marme   tel. 05 59 22 16 04   www.tabledaranda.fr/
Notes: €. "No problem." Many celiac clients.

Le Clos Basque   restaurant   Basque
12 avenue Louis Barthou   tel. 05 59 24 24 96
Notes: €€€ - €€€€. Advance notice necessary.

La Vie Claire   health food store   3 avenue Victor Hugo

BOE

Pre Vert 2   health food store   22 avenue de la Capelette

BORDEAUX

Croc Loup   restaurant   French
35 rue du Loupin (neighborhood rue Sainte Catherine)   tel. 05 56 44 21 19
http://www.crocloup.fr/
Notes: €€. Advance notice necessary.

Europa La Phenicienne   restaurant   Lebanese
54 rue du Palais Gallien   tel. 05 35 40 51 96
Notes: €€ - €€€

Jean Ramet   restaurant   French
7 place Jean Jaures   tel. 05 56 44 12 51
Notes: €€ - €€€€. They have many celiac clients and GF products on hand.
Must call in advance.

La Cape   restaurant   French
9 allee de la Morlette   tel. 05 57 80 24 25
Notes: €€ - €€€

Le Café Mouneyra   restaurant   café
118 rue Mouneyra   tel. 05 56 08 99 96   www.espace-mouneyra.com
Notes: €

Le Gabriel   restaurant   French
10 place de la Bourse   tel. 05 56 30 00 80   www.bordeaux-gabriel.fr
Notes: €€€€. "Yes of course." Advance notice.

L'Entrecote   restaurant   French
4 cours du 30 Juillet   tel. 05 56 81 76 10   www.entrecote.fr
Notes: €€

Biocoop Bordeaux Pasteur health food store   40/42 cours Pasteur
La Vie Claire   health food store   2 rue Croix Seguey

BRANTOME
Les Jardins Brantome   restaurant   French
33 rue de Mareuil   tel. 05 53 05 88 16   www.lesjardins-brantome.com/
Notes: €€€

CAHORS
Le Rendez-Vous   restaurant   French
49 rue Clement Marot   tel. 05 65 22 65 10
Notes: €€. Very nice stuff. Call the day you are coming they will make you a
GF dessert too!

L'Auberge du Vieux Cahors   Inn, restaurant   French
rue Saint-Urcisse 144   tel. 05 65 35 06 05   aubcahors.free.fr/
Notes: €€. Advance notice necessary.

CAUTERETS

Don Patillo   restaurant   Italian
22 rue Richelieu   tel. 05 62 42 58 71
Notes: €. Advance notice necessary.

La Grande Fache   restaurant   traditional French
5 rue Richelieu   tel. 06 08 93 76 30
Notes: N/A

CENON

Biocoop 4 Pavillons   health food store
213 avenue Carnot

CHANCELADE

Le Grain D'Or 3   health food store   Les Combeaux

CREYSSE

La Vie Claire   health food store
ZA La Nauve-134 avenue De La Roque

DAX CEDEX

Biocoop Sesame   health food store   18 boulevard Carnot BP 3

DIGNE LES BAINS

La Dormance   health food store   24 avenue du Maréchal Juin

DOMME

Le Saint Martial   restaurant   French
Le Bourg   tel. 05 53 29 18 34   http://www.lesaintmartial.com/
Notes: €€€€. Advance notice necessary.

EUGÉNIE-LES-BAINS

Les Prés d'Eugénie   hotel, restaurant   French
Landes   tel. 05 58 05 06 07   www.michelguerard.com
Notes: €€€€. GF dinner and breakfast.

GRADIGNAN

Saveur Et Nature   health food store   47 rue du Professeur Bernard

GUJAN MESTRAS

Le Grain De Ble   health food store   98 cours de Verdun

HAUTEFORT

La Table d'Erillac   restaurant   French
place Eugene Le Roy   tel. 05 53 51 61 49
Notes: € - €€. "Of course we can do it! We do it for many clients."

Auberge du Parc   hotel, restaurant, bar   French
place Rene Lavaud   tel. 05 53 50 88 98   www.aubergeduparc-hautefort.fr
Notes: €€. contact them in advance at aubergeduparc@free.fr

ISSIGEAC

Biocoop Issigeac   health food store   place de l'Eglise

JARNAC

'La Belle Demeure'   hotel/B&B
5 rue Virecourt   tel. 05 45 32 68 49   www.labelledemeure.com
Notes: N/A. Ultimate gluten-free accommodations. Never more than 10 guests.

La Vie Claire   health food store   2 Rue Portillon

LA ROQUE-GAGEAC

La Belle Etoile   hotel, restaurant   French
F-24250 La Roque-Gageac   tel. 05 53 29 51 44
www.hotel-belle-etoile-dordogne.fr
Notes: €€€ - €€€€

LE BOUSCAT

Delices Bio   health food store   141 boulevard Godard

LIBOURNE

Biocoop Libourne Nord   health food store
rue Firmin Didot Z.A Les Dagueys

Saison Bio   health food store   39 avenue de Verdun

LOURDES

Le Chalet de Biscaye   restaurant   French
26 Chemin du Lac   tel. 05 62 94 12 26
Notes: €€ - €€€

Le Magret   restaurant   French
10 rue des 4 Freres Soulas   tel. 05 62 94 20 55   www.lemagret.com
Notes: €€. "Yes, of course."

Maison du Cassoulet   restaurant   French
7 rue de la Grotte   tel. 05 62 42 38 70   www.maisonducassoulet.com/
Notes: €

MERIGNAC
Biocoop Merignac   health food store   72 ave Pierre Mendès Italie

MIREPEIX
Biocoop Des 4 Chemins   health food store   31 route de Lourdes

MONPAZIER
Restaurant Privilege du Perigord restaurant   French
58 rue Notre Dame   tel. 05 53 22 43 98   www.privilegeperigord.com/
Notes: €€€. Many celiac clients. Request GF in advance.

MONT DE MARSAN
La Vie Claire   health food store   240 avenue du Marechal Juin
Nature Et Sante   health food store   609 ave Président Kennedy

MONTPON MENESTEROL
Les Saveurs Du Potager health food store   avenue Jean Moulin

NONTRON
Biocoop Au P'Tit Bio   health food store   2 avenue Yvon Delbos

OLORON SAINTE MARIE
La Vie Claire   health food store   boulevard Des Pyrenees

ORAISON
Bioraison Centre Médico Social   health food store
8 bis rue Eugène Revest

ORTHEZ
La Vie Claire   health food store   26 avenue du 8 Mai

PAU
Au Fin Gourmet   restaurant   French
24 av Gaston Lacoste   tel. 05 59 27 47 71
www.restaurant-aufingourmet.com
Notes: €€€€

Buffalo Grill restaurant French
RN 117 2 avenue Alfred Nobel tel. 05 59 84 63 37 www.buffalo-grill.fr
Notes: € - €€. This restaurant chain has a list of foods which are allergen free and gluten-free.

El Mamounia restaurant Moroccan
9 rue des Orphelines tel. 05 59 27 12 44
Notes: € - €€. Some plates are already GF. Others they will adapt.

Le Bistrot d'a Cote restaurant traditional French
1 place Gramont tel. 05 59 27 98 08
Notes: €€

Le Dauphin restaurant French
place Etats tel. 05 59 27 80 48
Notes: € - €€

Le Gusto restaurant Italian
1 rue du Hedas tel. 05 59 98 43 77
http://www.restaurant-pau-gusto.com/restaurant-pau-bearn-aquitaine-sud-ouest.php
Notes: €€

Visnu restaurant Indian
20 rue Henri IV tel. 05 59 83 88 14
Notes: €€

La Vie Claire health food store 37 rue Emile Guichenne

PÉRIGUEUX

IZBA restaurant French
11 cours Fenelon tel. 05 53 09 37 51 izba.wifeo.com/
Notes: €

Le Bartola restaurant French
17 cours Fenelon tel. 05 53 54 99 02
Notes: €€ - €€€. Advance notice necessary.

Le Grain de Sel restaurant French
7 rue des Farges tel. 05 53 53 45 22
Notes: €€€

Le Rocher de l'Arsault   restaurant   French
15 rue Arsault   tel. 05 53 53 54 06   http://www.rocher-arsault.com/
Notes: €€ - €€€

L'Essentiel   restaurant   French
8 rue de la Clarte   tel. 05 53 35 15 15   restaurant-perigueux.com/
Notes: €€€€. "We don't use flour in our sauces."

La Vie Claire   health food store   15 rue Limogeanne
Le Grain D'Or   health food store   7 rue Salinière
PESSAC
Leon de Bruxelles   restaurant   Belgian
4 av Antoine Becquerel   tel. 02 51 89 05 06 www.leon-de-bruxelles.fr
Notes: €€€. This restaurant is part of a large chain all over France. They have
limited items that are GF, but their Director of Quality Control nationwide
provided us with a list of menu items that are GF. See page 16.

Saveur & Nature 2   health food store   44 av. Pierre Wiehn
PLAZAC
Le Mille-Feuilles   health food store   Le Cordestieux

PORT STE MARIE
Biocoop Gaïa   health food store   Le Ponchut RN 113

RIBERAC
Croq Sante   health food store   84 rue du 26 mars

ROCAMADOUR
Les Jardins de la Louve   restaurant   French
place Hugon - La Cite   tel. 05 65 33 62 93   http://www.rocamadour.com
Notes: N/A. Advance notice necessary.

SAINT ANDRE DE CUBZAC
La Vie Claire   health food store   230 route De Libourne
SAINT EMILION
L'Envers du Decor   restaurant   French, wine bar
11 rue du Clocher   tel. 05 57 74 48 31   www.envers-dudecor.com/
Notes: N/A

L'Hostellerie de Plaisance   hotel, restaurant   French
3 place du Clocher   tel. 05 57 55 07 55   www.hostellerie-plaisance.com
Notes: €€€€

SAINT JEAN DE LUZ

La Vie Claire   health food store   140 avenue De Jalday

SAINT VINCENT DE TYROSSE

Biocoop De Châlons   health food store
Zone Commerciale de Châlons – rue des Lauriers

SARLAT LA CANEDA

Chez Le Gaulois   restaurant   French
1 rue de Tourny   tel. 05 53 59 50 64
Notes: €. Advance notice necessary.

Criquettamu's   restaurant   French
5 rue Armes   tel. 05 53 59 48 10   www.criquettamus.fr
Notes: €€

Le Bistro de l'Octroi   restaurant   French
111 avenue Selves   tel. 05 53 30 83 40   http://lebistrodeloctroi.fr/
Notes: €€. "Yes, absolutely."

Les Jardins d'Harmonie   restaurant   French regional, modern
place Andre Malraux   tel. 05 53 31 06 69
http://www.lesjardinsdharmonie.com/
Notes: €€€ - €€€€. The staff is very accommodating. Ask for Chef Marc.

Restaurant Le Grand Bleu   restaurant   French
43 avenue de la Gare   tel. 05 53 31 08 48   http://www.legrandbleu.eu/
Notes: €€€€

SAUVETERRE-DE-BÉARN

La Maison de Navarre   hotel, restaurant   French
Quartier Saint-Marc   tel. 05 59 38 55 28   la-maison-de-navarre.com
Notes: €€€€

ST CYBRANET

La Belle Demeure   B&B   French
Lieu-Dit Le Bouscot   tel. 05 53 28 57 12   www.Labelledemeure.Com
Notes: €€€€. Specializes in gluten-free.

ST-JEAN-PIED-DE-PORT

Piramide Le Relais   hotel, restaurant   French
19 place du Général-de-Gaulle   tel. 05 59 37 01 01
www.relaischateaux.com/en/search-book/hotel-restaurant/pyrenees/
Notes: €€€€. GF breakfast and dinner.

TERRASSON

La Vie Claire   health food store
place De La Mairie-10 avenue Charles De Gaulle

TRELISSAC

Le Grain D'Or 2   health food store   120 av. Michel Grandou

VILLARS

Château de Villars   hotel/B&B   French
Pres de la Cure   tel. 05 53 03 41 58   www.chateaudevillars.com/fr
Notes: €€€€. Every kind of accommodation you can imagine, and gluten free food

VILLENAVE D'ORNON

Leon de Bruxelles   restaurant   Belgian
3 rue Lino Ventura   tel. 02 43 27 41 49   www.leon-de-bruxelles.fr
Notes: €€€. This restaurant is part of a large chain all over France. They have limited items that are GF, but their Director of Quality Control nationwide provided us with a list of menu items that are GF. See page 16.

Saveur Et Nature   health food store   42 rue Pagès

FRANCHE-COMTE (FRANCHE-COMTÉ)

Les Americains en France (M. Katzman)

ARBOIS

Chateau de Germigney   restaurant   French
Hotel du Parc   tel. 03 84 73 85 85
Notes: €€€€. Advance notice necessary.

Restaurant La Cuisance   restaurant   French
62 place de Faramand   tel. 03 84 37 40 74   http://www.lacuisance.fr/
Notes: €€. Advance notice necessary.

BELFORT

Desperado-Cactus   restaurant   Mexican
22 rue Michelet   tel. 03 84 26 79 36
Notes: €€. Advance notice necessary.

La Gazelle d'or   restaurant   Moroccan
4 rue Quatre Vents   tel. 03 84 58 02 87
http://www.lagazelledor.fr/gazelle-or.php
Notes: €. Advance notice necessary.

L'Ambroisie   restaurant   French
2 place Grande Fontaine   tel. 03 84 28 67 00
Notes: €€. Advance notice necessary.

La Vie Claire   health food store   138 avenue Jean Jaurès
Le Grenier Vert   health food store   4 bis rue du Comte de la Suze

BESANÇON

Bêtises et Volup'thé   restaurant   Bio/vegetarian
79 rue des Granges   tel. 03 81 50 83 45   betises-et-volupthe.fr
Notes: N/A

Brasserie 1802   restaurant   French
place Granvelle   tel. 03 81 82 21 97   http://www.besac.com/1802/
Notes: €€. Advance notice necessary.

Le Taj Mahal   restaurant   Indian
9 rue Claude Pouillet   tel. 03 81 81 98 71
Notes: €€€. many celiac clients.

Leon de Bruxelles restaurant Belgian
rue René Char tel. 02 31 83 05 25 www.leon-de-bruxelles.fr
Notes: €€€. This restaurant is part of a large chain all over France. They have limited items that are GF, but their Director of Quality Control nationwide provided us with a list of menu items that are GF. See page 16.

Mirabelle restaurant bio
1 rue Megevand tel. 03 81 50 10 20
Notes: €. Advance notice necessary.

Poker d'As Le restaurant French
14 Clos Saint Amour tel. 03 81 81 42 49
http://www.restaurant-lepokerdas.fr/
Notes: €€€ - €€€€. Advance notice necessary.

Biocoop La Canopee health food store 3 allée de l'Ile aux Moineaux

CHALEZEULE
La Vie Claire health food store 1 route Nationale
FOIX
Biocoop Mirabelle health food store 20 rue Saint Vincent

LES ROUSSES
Biocoop Du Haut Jura health food store
191 route du Génie – Zone artisanale des Adraits

LONS LE SAUNIER
La Comedie restaurant French
65 place Comedie tel. 03 84 24 20 66
Notes: €€€. Advance notice necessary.

Le Comptoir du Mirabilis restaurant French
9 Galerie Lecourbe tel. 03 84 25 96 37
http://www.lecomptoirdumirabilis.com/
Notes: €€. Advance notice necessary.

LUXEUIL
La Vie Claire health food store 5 Allée Maroselli

MONTBELIARD
Chez Cass'Graine restaurant fusion
4 rue du General Leclerc tel. 03 81 91 09 97
Notes: €€ - €€€€. Advance notice necessary.

La Table de Marie   restaurant   French
4 rue du Chateau   tel. 03 81 91 27 58 perso.orange.fr/la-table-de-marie
Notes: €€€ - €€€€. Advance notice necessary.

MONTMOROT/LONS
La Vie Claire   health food store   12 ave Pasteur route de Lyon

MORTEAU
La Vie Claire   health food store   7 rue del la Gare

PONTARLIER
Biocoop Du Haut Doubs health food store   9 rue Arthur Bourdin

SAINT CLAUDE
La Vie Claire   health food store
ZA Etables rue de la Pierre qu vire (A côté de Défimode)

VESOUL
Biosaone   health food store
Zone commerciale Espace de la Motte 3 rueTallerot

La Vie Claire   health food store   50 boulevard des Alliés

La Tour de France

LIMOUSIN(LIMOUSIN)

CHERVES DE COGNAC B-B
14, Chemin des Basses rues
16370 Cherves Richemont
Contact: Tina Dower
tel. 06 32 50 19 46
www.glutenfreefrance.com

A luxuriously-appointed, beautifully
renovated farmhouse with optional
half-board accommodation near
Cognac in the Limousin region featuring:

• 10m x 6m heated swimming pool.
• **Gluten free cooking a speciality.**
• 3 large double bedrooms, with private facilities. Accommodates up to 6 adults and 5 children.
• Walk to village bar, restaurant, boulangerie and charcuterie.
• Gated walled garden with ample parking, some covered.
• Pool house with 'honesty' drinks fridge, w/c and shower.
• Large shady terrace with barbecue overlooking the pool.
• An ideal base for exploring the Charente, or as a touring stopover.
•Satellite TV, DVD library, HiFi with iPod link & WiFi Broadband.
• From €60 per night B&B. Minimum stay: 2 nights.

Gluten Free meals
Having a celiac in the family means that creative cooking is a way of life.
• Picnics and afternoon tea & cakes on request.
• Alfresco, BBQ's, casual dining & evening meals
• A four course dinner is €35 each. Three courses for €30 each.

Typical Menu (please request in advance)
Apéritif - Pineau / Kir
Starter - Warm Goats Cheese Salad / Moules Marinière
Main - Chicken breast stuffed with prunes / Roast cod with pesto crust, dauphinoise potatoes, green beans & roasted carrots
Wine - Grand vin de Bordeaux
Cheese - Local platter with French bread
Dessert - Apple Tarte Tatin or Vanilla Cheesecake
Coffee/Tea - Cognac or Liqueurs (extra)

ARNAC POMPADOUR

Club Med Pompadour   all-inclusive resort   French
Domaine De La Noaille   tel. 05 55 97 30 00
http://www.clubmed.com/cm/jsp/clubmed_welcome.jsp
Notes: €€€€

BEAULIEU-SUR-DORDOGNE

Le Manoir de Beaulieu   restaurant   French
4 place du Champ de Mars   tel. 05 55 91 01 34
www.manoirdebeaulieu.com
Notes: €€€

Grand Hotel le Turenne   hotel/restaurant   French
1 Blvd. St. Rodolphe de Turenne   tel. 05 55 91 94 72
Notes: €€€€. They already have many celiac clients. Can serve GF breakfast and dinner. Just request when you come.

BRIVE-LA-GAILLARDE

Restaurant Les Viviers Saint Martin   restaurant   French
4 rue Traversiere   tel. 05 55 92 14 15   http://www.les-viviers.fr/
Notes: €€€

Truffe Noire   restaurant   French
22 boulevard Anatole France   tel. 05 55 92 45 00
Notes: €€ - €€€€

Hotel/Restaurant La Cremaillere   hotel/restaurant   French
53 avenue de Paris   tel. 05 55 74 32 47
www.la-cremaillere-brive.e-monsite.com
Notes: €€€€. GF breakfast, lunch, dinner. E-mail request in advance.

CHERVES RICHEMONT

Cherves De Cognac B-B   B&B   French
14 Chemin Des Basses rues   tel. 06 32 50 19 46
www.glutenfreefrance.com
Notes: €€€. Specializes in gluten-free.

FEYTIAT

Biocoop Feytiat   health food store   2 avenue Martial Valin

GUERET

La Vie Claire   health food store   4 rue de l'Eglise

LIMOGES

Chez Alphonse restaurant French
5 place Motte tel. 05 55 34 34 14
Notes: €€€. Advance notice necessary.

Le Croquembouche restaurant French
14 rue Haute Cite tel. 05 55 33 17 54
Notes: €

Le Versailles restaurant French
20 place Aine tel. 05 55 34 13 39
Notes: €€ - €€€€. Advance notice necessary.

La Vie Claire health food store 9 rue Lansecot

ORADOUR-SUR-VAYRES

Restaurant La Bergerie restaurant French
Chemin de la Cote tel. 05 55 78 29 91
Notes: €€€. Advance notice necessary.

ROCHECHOUART

Le Roc du Boeuf restaurant French
Le Moulin de la Cote | route de Babaudus tel. 05 55 03 61 75
http://www.lerocduboeuf.com
Notes: €€€

SADROC

Le Relais du Bas Limousin restaurant French
RN 20 La Fonsalade tel. 05 55 84 52 06
www.relaisbaslimousin.fr/restaurant.html
Notes: €€ - €€€. Advance notice necessary.

SAINT JEAN PIED DE PORT

Les Pyrénées restaurant French
19 place du Général-de-Gaulle tel. 05 59 37 01 01
http://www.relaischateaux.com/en/search-book/hotel-restaurant/pyrenees/
Notes: €€€€. GF breakfast and dinner. Restaurant is in the hotel Piramide.

TURENNE

Le Vieux Sechoir restaurant French
Gare tel. 05 55 85 90 46
Notes: €€

Paul Farla restaurant French
Bourg tel. 05 55 85 91 32
Notes: N/A. English spoken. Call ahead.

Fayrac Manor, Beynac (Kollin)

NORTH-CALAIS
(NORD-PAS-DE-CALAIS)

Eglise (R. Levy)

AULNOY LEZ VALENCIENNES

Leon de Bruxelles   restaurant   Belgian
rue Jules Mousseron Autoroute A2 sortie 21a:Universite Mont Houy
tel. 03 27 21 58 01   www.leon-de-bruxelles.fr
Notes: €€€. This restaurant is part of a large chain all over France. They have
limited items that are GF, but their Director of Quality Control nationwide
provided us with a list of menu items that are GF. See page 16.

AVESNES SUR HELPE

El Tout Bio   health food store   1 rue Prisse d'Avenne

BOULOGNE SUR MER

Opale Bio Biocoop   health food store   17 rue Edmond Rostand

CALAIS

Buffalo Grill   restaurant   French
avenue Roger Salengro   tel. 03 21 96 40 70   www.buffalo-grill.fr
Notes: € - €€. This restaurant chain has a list of foods which are allergen-free
and gluten-free.

CALAIS

La Buissonnière   restaurant   French
10 rue Neuve   tel. 03 21 96 22 32 http://restaurant-calais.com/cariboost1
Notes: €€€ - €€€€

La Vie Claire   health food store   9 rue du Duc de Guise

CAMBRAI

La Vie Claire   health food store   4 rue d'Alger
Vitavie   health food store   cal Elysée quartier Martin Martine

CAPINGHEM

Biocoop Bio Et'Hique   health food store   8 rue Poincaré

HAZEBROUCK

Bioambiance   health food store   6 avenue de la Haute Loge

LEZENNES

Leon de Bruxelles   restaurant   Belgian
rue de Chanzy   tel. 03 20 91 49 51   www.leon-de-bruxelles.fr
Notes: €€€. This restaurant is part of a large chain all over France. They have
limited items that are GF, but their Director of Quality Control nationwide
provided us with a list of menu items that are GF. See page 16.

LILLE

Restaurant La Source   restaurant   organic/bio
13 rue du Plat   tel. 03 20 57 53 07   www.denislasource.com
Notes: €

EXKi Lille - Rue Nationale   Fast, healthy food   Fast, healthy food
70 rue Nationale   www.exki.fr
Notes: . Some dishes have been labeled "SF" or "sans gluten."

EXKi Lille- Grand Place   Fast, healthy food   Fast, healthy food
9 place Rihour   www.exki.fr
Notes: . Some dishes have been labeled "SF" or "sans gluten."

La Vie Claire   health food store   34 ave Charles Saint Venant
Label Vie   health food store   98 rue de Solferino

MARCQ EN BAROEUL

Label Vie   health food store   101 bd Clemenceau

MAUBEUGE

El Tout Bio Maubeuge   health food store   15 boulevard de l'Epinette

NOYELLES GODAULT

Leon de Bruxelles   restaurant   Belgian
RN 43 - avenue de la République   tel. 03 83 21 16 63
www.leon-de-bruxelles.fr
Notes: €€€. This restaurant is part of a large chain all over France. They have
limited items that are GF, but their Director of Quality Control nationwide
provided us with a list of menu items that are GF. See page 16.

RONCQ

Cooking & Cie   Catering
185 rue de Lille   tel. 06 48 07 83 44   lacompagniesansgluten.com
Notes: € - €€

RONCQ

Biovalys   health food store   495 rue de Lille

SECLIN

La Dolce Vita   restaurant-pizzéria   world cuisine
25 place Paul Eluard   tel. 03 20 97 07 7 www.geocities.com/resto_dolcevita
Notes: €

La Vie Claire   health food store   rue Sadi Carnot

VALENCIENNES

Biocoop Valenciennes   health food store   22 rue Ernest Macarez

VILLENEUVE D'ASCQ

Leon de Bruxelles   restaurant   Belgian
Centre Cial V2 Bid Valmy   tel. 03 20 47 85 73 www.leon-de-bruxelles.fr
Notes: €€€. This restaurant is part of a large chain all over France. They have
limited items that are GF, but their Director of Quality Control nationwide
provided us with a list of menu items that are GF. See page 16.

Saveurs Et Saisons   health food store   270 rue des Fusillés

WASQUEHAL

Leon de Bruxelles   restaurant   Belgian
Av Grand Cottignies   tel. 03 20 72 66 34   www.leon-de-bruxelles.fr
Notes: €€€. This restaurant is part of a large chain all over France. They have
limited items that are GF, but their Director of Quality Control nationwide
provided us with a list of menu items that are GF. See page 16.

Label Vie Wasquehal   health food store   51 avenue de Flandres

WAVRIN

Vert'Tige   health food store   rue Anatole France

WAZEMMES

Vert'Tige   health food store   Marché couvert place Nouvelle Aventure

PICARDY(PICARDIE)

Saint-Valery-sur-Somme

ABBEVILLE
Buffalo Grill   restaurant   French
Parc d'Activités des 2 Vallées   tel. 03 22 20 53 56   www.buffalo-grill.fr
Notes: € - €€. This restaurant chain has a list of foods which are allergen-free
and gluten-free.

AGNETZ
Auberge de Gicourt   restaurant   French
466 av.Philippe Courtial   tel. 03 44 50 00 31
www.aubergedegicourt.com/contact.html
Notes: €€ - €€€€. "No problem! Just come."

ALBERT
Hotel de la Paix Restaurant   restaurant   French
43 rue Victor-Hugo   tel. 03 22 75 01 64
Notes: €€€€

La Vie Claire   health food store   51 rue de Birmingham

BEAUVAIS
Leon de Bruxelles   restaurant   Belgian
ZAC du Pinconlieu Angle Salvador Allende   tel. 03 81 87 08 07
www.leon-de-bruxelles.fr
Notes: €€€. This restaurant is part of a large chain all over France. They have
limited items that are GF, but their Director of Quality Control nationwide
provided us with a list of menu items that are GF. See page 16.

Biocoop Beauvais   health food store   288 ter rue de Clermont

BERRY AU BAC
Cote 108 La   restaurant   French
1 rue Colonel Vergezac   tel. 03 23 79 95 04   www.lacote108.com/
Notes: €€€ - €€€€. Advance notice necessary.

CREIL
Biocoop Creil   health food store   1118 ave du Tremblay

DURY
L'Aubergade   restaurant   French
78 route Nationale   tel. 03 22 89 51 41   www.aubergade-dury.com
Notes: €€€€. Advance notice necessary.

GLISY

Leon de Bruxelles   restaurant   Belgian
avenue de la Ville Idéale   tel. 01 30 37 49 40   www.leon-de-bruxelles.fr
Notes: €€€. This restaurant is part of a large chain all over France. They have limited items that are GF, but their Director of Quality Control nationwide provided us with a list of menu items that are GF. See page 16.

GOUVIEUX

La Renardiere   restaurant   French
2 rue Freres Segard   tel. 03 44 57 08 23
http://www.restaurantlarenardiere.fr/
Notes: €€€€. Reservations necessary. Request GF.

LA FERTE-MILON

Les Ruines   restaurant   French fusion
14 rue du Vieux Chateau   tel. 03 23 96 71 56   www.lesruines.com
Notes: €€ - €€€

LE CROTOY

Hotel-Restaurant l'Hotel de la Dune   hotel/restaurant   French
1352 rue de la Dune   tel. 03 22 25 01 88
http://www.auberge-de-la-dune.com
Notes: €€€ - €€€€. GF breakfast too.

L'Auberge de la Marine Restaurant   hotel/restaurant   French
1 rue Florentin Lefils   tel. 03 22 27 92 44   www.aubergedelamarine.com
Notes: €€ - €€€. English spoken. "Just come." Many celiac guests.

MARGNY LES COMPIEGNE

Comptoir Bio   health food store
Rés. Raymond Poincarré 208 rue Molière

QUEND

Le Fiacre   restaurant   French
6 rue des Pommiers   tel. 03 22 23 47 30   www.lefiacre.fr
Notes: €€€ - €€€€. "Yes, of course" advance notice necessary.

ROYE

La Flamiche   restaurant   French
place de L'Hotel de Ville   tel. 03 22 87 00 56   www.laflamiche.fr
Notes: €

SAINT JEAN AUX BOIS

La Fontaine Saint Jean   restaurant   French
21 rue des Plaideurs   tel. 03 44 42 18 12   www.la-fontaine-saint-jean.com
Notes: €€. Very knowledgeable about GF. Many celiac clients. Reservations necessary; you can request GF when you get there.

SAINT MAXIMIN

Leon de Bruxelles   restaurant   Belgian
ZAC du Bois des Fenêtres - 790 rue Louis St Just   tel. 03 83 21 16 63
www.leon-de-bruxelles.fr
Notes: €€€. This restaurant is part of a large chain all over France. They have limited items that are GF, but their Director of Quality Control nationwide provided us with a list of menu items that are GF. See page 16.

SAINT QUENTIN

Buffalo Grill   restaurant   French
ZAC du Bois de la Chocque avenue Lavoisier   tel. 03 23 67 10 24
www.buffalo-grill.fr
Notes: € - €€. This restaurant chain has a list of foods which are allergen-free and gluten-free.

Delices d'Envies   restaurant   traditional French
37 rue Raspail   tel. 03 23 60 93 14
Notes: N/A. Many celiac clients.

La Vie Bio   health food store   13 bis bd Gambetta
La Vie Claire   health food store   21 rue Emile Zola

SAINT VALERY SUR SOMME

Le Nicol's   restaurant   French
15 rue Ferte   tel. 03 22 26 82 96
http://alain.leduc.pagesperso-orange.fr/index.htm
Notes: €€. Please indicate GF needs when you make reservations.

VRON

Clos du Moulin   hotel, restaurant   French
3 rue du Marechal Leclerc   tel. 03 22 23 74 75   www.leclosdumoulin.fr
Notes: €€ - €€€. **Extensive gluten-free menu!!!

LE CLOS DU MOULIN
The atmosphere of old times ... the comfort of today.
Hostellerie-Restaurant
Sample gluten-free menu

Starters without gluten
Terrine of foie gras cooked with dried apricots
Royal salad of the clos (with mushrooms, salmon, pesto, pepper, goat tomette mackerel)
"Uncertain" white asparagus of Picardy (cooking according to season and production)
Seared Red Mullet with Orange and vegetables
Trio of Prawns on apple remoulade and beansprouts
Marinated chicken and fried sweet potatoes
Picardy string of Countess Clos to chestnut flour (a "bio" taste discovery)

Gluten-free main dishes
Sliced fresh salmon
Medallions of Monkfish with yellow fruits and beet juice
Tab of the local butcher and braised shallots
Secret room farmhouse stuffed mushrooms-peppers (old secret recipe)
Seared Filet of Beef by Marc with crayfish tails
Cassolette of Lamb at thePaimpol cocos cooked the "tagine" way

Gluten free desserts
The slate of the 3 cheeses (choice depending on availability)
Creme Brulee "Christopher" (with chicory and violet)
Baked Alaska House flavor of the day
Fresh fruit salad (order at the beginning of the meal)
Soufflé à l'orange (order at the beginning of the meal)

Gluten free breakfast
Omelet (single, mushrooms, cheese or ham)
Eggs (scrambled or fried)
Mini baguette
Full sliced bread
Pain au chocolate
Croissant

POITOU-CHARENTES
(POITOU-CHARENTES)

Voici les fleurs (I. Briton)

Le Chêne Vert B&B
34 rue des Abatis, Chez Primo
17770 Burie, France
Contact person: Lynne & Steve
Adams
tel: 05 46 90 66 96
E-mail:
lynneadams34@hotmail.com

Bed and Breakfast accommodation in a "Maison Charentaise" at Burie
Near Cognac and Saintes, in Charente Maritime, France

Cognac, with many distilleries, and the Romanesque town of Saintes are a
short drive away. There are four golf courses in the area and lots of
opportunity for fishing and cycling. In less than an hour you can be at the
sandy beaches of the Gironde estuary. The quiet roads, vineyard lanes and
woodland paths are perfect for a gentle stroll and a little farther walk leads to
the 12th century Abbaye de Fontdouce.

Evening dinner is prepared using fresh local produce. **Gluten-free and
vegetarian meals are prepared on request.**

Each of four guest rooms has a fully tiled en-suite shower room. There are
three double rooms and one twin room.

ANGOULEME

Restaurant La ruelle   restaurant   gastropub
6 rue des Trois Notre-Dame   tel. 05 45 95 15 19
www.restaurant-laruelle.com/index.php
Notes: €€€€. English spoken. Call ahead.

Biocoop Vitamine   health food store   467 route de Bordeaux
Brin D'Aillet   health food store   198 rue Alfred de Vigny

ANGOULINS

Buffalo Grill   restaurant   French
Les Cadélis Est RN 137   tel. 05 46 56 94 00   www.buffalo-grill.fr
Notes: € - €€. This restaurant chain has a list of foods which areallergen free
and gluten-free.

Regain Sud   health food store   ZAC des Fourneaux

ARS-EN-RE

Grenier a Sel Le   restaurant   French
20 Chemin Baie   tel. 05 46 29 08 62   http://www.grenierasel.fr/
Notes: €€. English spoken. Many celiac clients.

BASSAC

Auberge de Conde   restaurant   French
rue Rixendis Loriches   tel. 05 45 83 09 67   www.auberge-de-conde.net
Notes: € - €€

BRESSUIRE

Biocoop Bressuire   health food store   4 rue de l'Espace

BURIE

Le Chêne Vert   B&B   French
34 rue Des Abatis Chez Primo   tel. 05 46 90 66 96
Lynneadams34@hotmail.Com
Notes: Specializes in gluten-free.

CHALAIS

Biocoop Chalais   health food store   38 rue de Barbezieux

CHATEAUBERNARD

Biocoop Pays De Cognac health food store   8 rue du Poitou

CHATELLERAULT

Le Pois Tout Vert   health food store
Zone d'Argenson - 2 rue d'Arsonval

CHAURAY

Biocoop Le Baquet Vert   health food store
Zone commerciale Chauray - Bd Ampère

COGNAC

La Braserade   restaurant   French
23 rue Pont Faumet   tel. 05 45 82 00 45
Notes: N/A

Le Fair Play   restaurant   French
25 rue Henri Fichon   tel. 05 45 82 57 35
Notes: N/A. Extremely nice staff.

COULONGES SUR L'AUTIZE

Le Plantivore   health food store   27 rue du Commerce

GOND-PONTOUVRE

Epicea   health food store   69 route de Paris

LA FLOTTE

Chai Nous Comme Chai Vous   restaurant   bistro
1 rue Garde   tel. 05 46 09 49 85
chainouscommechaivous.over-blog.com/
Notes: €€€ - €€€€

L'Ecailler   restaurant   French
3 Quai Senac   tel. 05 46 09 56 40   www.lecailler-iledere.com
Notes: €€€. Advance notice necessary. Very nice staff.

LA ROCHELLE

La Rose des Vins   restaurant   Bistro
16 rue Cloutiers   tel. 05 46 41 87 43
http://www.restaurant-larosedesvins.com/
Notes: N/A. Advance notice necessary.

L'Annexe   restaurant   French
45 rue St Nicolas   tel. 05 46 50 67 71
Notes: €€. "Just come."

Le Comptoir des Voyages restaurant International
22 rue Saint-Jean-du-Perot   tel. 05 46 50 62 60
www.lecomptoirdesvoyages.com
Notes: €€. Make reservations one week in advance.

Les Flots restaurant French
1 rue de la Chaine   tel. 05 46 41 32 51   www.les-flots.com
Notes: €€€€. "No problem!" English spoken. Advance notice necessary.

LA ROCHE-POSAY
Restaurant Saint-Roch restaurant French
4 cours Pasteur   tel. 05 49 19 49 45
www.resorthotel-larocheposay.fr/restaurant-gastro...
Notes: €€€. "Just come."

LAGORD / LA ROCHELLE
Regain health food store   297 avenue des Corsaires

LE CHATEAU D'OLERON
Les Jardins d'Alienor restaurant French
7-11 rue Marechal Foch   tel. 05 46 76 48 30   www.lesjardinsdalienor.com
Notes: €€

LES MATHES
Club Med La Palmyre Atlantique all-inclusive resort French
Allee du Grand Large   tel. 05 46 39 77 30   www.clubmed.fr
Notes: €€€€

LOUDUN
Le Ricordeau restaurant French
6 place Boeufferie   tel. 05 49 22 67 27
Notes: € - €€. Advance notice necessary.

MARENNES
Le Cayenne restaurant French
19 rue des Martyrs   tel. 05 46 85 01 06
Notes: €€. Advance notice necessary.

MESCHERS-SUR-GIRONDE
La Foret restaurant French
64 rte Royan   tel. 05 46 02 79 87
http://www.restaurantlaforet1.com/printversion.html
Notes: €€€ - €€€€. Advance notice necessary.

MONCONTOUR

Le Chaudron Magique   restaurant   French
1 place de la Carriere   tel. 02 96 73 40 34   www.le-chaudron-magique.com
Notes: €€. Reservations necessary. Ask for GF meal when you make
reservations.

NIORT

Buffalo Grill   restaurant   French
Espace Mendes France 23 rue de Condorcet   tel. 05 49 33 40 64
www.buffalo-grill.fr
Notes: € - €€. This restaurant chain has a list of foods which are allergen-free
and gluten-free.

L'Adresse   restaurant   French
247 avenue La Rochelle   tel. 05 49 79 41 06
Notes: €€. "Just come."

PARTHENAY

Restaurant Les Deux Epis   restaurant   Bistro
47 rue Jean Jaures   tel. 05 49 64 13 33
Notes: €€. English spoken.

POITIERS

La Table du Jardin   restaurant   French fusion
42 rue Moulin a Vent   tel. 05 49 41 68 46   www.latabledujardin.com
Notes: €€

Le Bistro de l'Absynthe   restaurant   French
36 rue Carnot   tel. 05 49 37 28 44
Notes: €€. Advance notice necessary.

Taverne de Maitre Kanter   restaurant   Seafood
24 rue Carnot   tel. 05 49 50 10 80   http://www.tmk-poitiers.com/
Notes: € - €€

La Vie Claire   health food store   40 rue Magenta
Le Pois Tout Vert   health food store   20 route de Bonneuil Matours

Le Pois Tout Vert Demie Lune   health food store
55 ave du Plateau des Glières

Le Pois Tout Vert Porte Sud   health food store
Centre commercial Porte Sud - 204 avenue du 8mai 1945

PORT-DES-BARQUES

La Chaloupe   restaurant   Seafood
49 avenue de l'Ile Madame   tel. 05 46 83 00 10
http://www.lachaloupe17.com/
Notes: €€

PUILBOREAU

La Vie Claire   health food store   7 rue du 8 mai - ZAC de Beaulieu

ROCHEFORT

Biocoop Rochefort   health food store   rue des Pêcheurs d'Islande

ROYAN

L'Aquarelle   restaurant   French
22 rte de Cande | Breuillet   tel. 05 46 22 11 38
http://www.laquarelle.net/accueil.html
Notes: €€ - €€€. Advance notice necessary. When you are there ask to speak
to the shelf.

Restaurant Resto Lounge Le 61   restaurant   Seafood
61 avenue de Paris   tel. 05 46 39 01 01   www.le61chaumiere.com
Notes: €€ - €€€

SAINT JEAN D'ANGELY

L'Annexe   restaurant   Seafood
place du Pilori   tel. 05 46 32 28 28
Notes: €€ - €€€

SAINT MARTIN DEL RE

Cote Jardin   restaurant   French
14 rue Emile Atgier   tel. 05 46 68 16 75   www.restocotejardin.fr
Notes: €. "Yes, absolutely. Just come."

SAINT PIERRE D'OLERON

Le Petit Coivre   restaurant   French
10 avenue de Bel Air   tel. 05 46 47 13 77   www.lepetitcoivre.fr/
Notes: € - €€

Le Zing   restaurant   French
1 rue Louis Barthou   tel. 05 46 47 02 08
Notes: €€ - €€€. They have many items on the menu that GF. "Just come."

SAINT SAVIN

Restaurant Cadieu   restaurant   French
15 rue du Bourg Neuf   tel. 05 49 48 17 69   www.cadieu-86.com/index.php
Notes: € - €€. Advance notice necessary.

SAINTES

Le Parvis   restaurant   French
12-12 bis quai de l'Yser   tel. 05 46 97 78 12
http://www.restaurant-le-parvis.fr/
Notes: €€ - €€€. Just call the day of your visit, after 5pm to let them know.

SAUJON

Le Menestrel   restaurant   French
2 place Richelieu   tel. 05 46 06 92 35
http://www.restaurant-lemenestrel.com/
Notes: €€€ - €€€€. "Of course!". Advance notice necessary.

VAUX SUR MER

Biocoop Du Pays Royannais Za   health food store
du Plain 16 rue Georges Claude

VELLÈCHES

La Table des écoliers   restaurant   French
1 bis rue de l'étang   tel. 05 49 93 35 51   www.latabledesecoliers.com
Notes: €. Very aware of GF issues.

VIENNE

La Pyramide   restaurant   French
14 bd. Fernand-Point   tel. 04 74 53 01 96   www.lapyramide.com
Notes: €€€€. Very willing to make GF dishes.

L'Arlequin   restaurant   French
9 rue Clercs   tel. 04 74 31 78 10
Notes: €€ - €€€

Le Bec Fin   restaurant   regional
7 place St. Maurice   tel. 04 74 85 76 72
Notes: €€€€. Very willing to make GF dishes.

Restaurant Restique   restaurant   French
16 rue Boson   tel. 04 74 85 48 65
Notes: N/A. Many celiac clients and many celiac products.

INDEX

Aix (J. Friedman)

B

G

H

M

T